Lessons of Nature
FROM A MODERN-DAY SHEPHERD

Don F. Pickett

authorHOUSE®

AuthorHouse™
1663 Liberty Drive
Bloomington, IN 47403
www.authorhouse.com
Phone: 1 (800) 839-8640

Published by AuthorHouse 01/13/2018

ISBN: 978-1-5462-2016-9 (sc)
ISBN: 978-1-5462-2014-5 (hc)
ISBN: 978-1-5462-2015-2 (e)

Library of Congress Control Number: 2017918670

Print information available on the last page.

Any people depicted in stock imagery provided by Thinkstock are models, and such images are being used for illustrative purposes only. Certain stock imagery © Thinkstock.

This book is printed on acid-free paper.

Because of the dynamic nature of the Internet, any web addresses or links contained in this book may have changed since publication and may no longer be valid. The views expressed in this work are solely those of the author and do not necessarily reflect the views of the publisher, and the publisher hereby disclaims any responsibility for them.

All biblical scriptures were taken from the King James Version of The Bible – Public Domain.

Contents

To the Youth of America

For sixty centuries, people who have populated this earth have witnessed the lessons of nature, God's perfect order of harmony, beauty, magnificence, and grandeur.

During this millennium, these lessons have become lost and rediscovered with the falling and the rising of humanity.

> There'd be no corruption, there'd be no crime
>> without nature's law transgressed.
> A world in disruption is harvest time
>> for people to be depressed.

The physical creations of God, including ourselves and the world in which we live, are patterned after Him and show us how He functions in a perfect state of existence. Consequently, the whole of your life's decisions will surely be met with the appropriate reward or punishment, all depending on how well you adhere to His teachings as our Creator.

In the firm faith that these thoughts from *Lessons of Nature from a Modern-Day Shepherd* can elevate the quality of your lives, this work is dedicated to you.

Introduction

And behold, all things have their likeness,
and all things are created and made to
bear record of me, both things which are
temporal, and things which are spiritual.

(Moses 6:63)

Billions of God's children have inhabited this earth with no understanding of how to read or write. Nature is God's handiwork and is yet another method He uses to express His will to His children throughout the universe. The beauty and harmony of the planets within their spheres are the result of His omniscient intelligence and wisdom. Earth's day and night, summer and winter, seed time and harvest, are all manifestations of the regularity, beauty, order, and harmony of God's wisdom and love.

God arranged our universe
as a token of His love.
All humankind can now rehearse
as His guidance from above.

Lesson 1

A Shepherd's Vision

Those loyal shepherds in Chaldea
      while watching their flocks at night
would probe the dark panacea
      and find their way in God's sight.

Today the modern idea
      is a different source of light,
to overcome darkness via
      electrical power sites.

For modern academia
      and the students they incite,
forget the men of Judea,
      in fog they blindly unite.

Like Pilate in Caesarea
      his Savior did extradite,
the billboards and the media
      call mistake and sin all right.

A spiritual diarrhea
      can certainly be our plight
but urea is urea
      it ruins God's appetite.

Imagine yourself lost in a wild and strange country, all alone in a dark and secluded place, far from home and family. How will you cope emotionally? How can you find comfort and security? Is there anything you can rely on to find your way home? Can you even determine which way is north, south, east, or west? Such a situation is not uncommon for shepherds, who have concern not only for themselves but also for the animals over which they are given great responsibility and accountability.

Fortunately for the typical shepherd, experience has taught him that he is not alone. While his sheep graze peacefully along a hillside and his dogs walk complacently at his side, all nature seems to accept him as part of her own, and he knows he is in good company. Clearly he understands that he is not without risk or adversity, but he also knows that so long as his life is in harmony with his Creator, he will be protected.

An ancient Islamic story tells of an old man who invested all his money on his young son's education by sending him to school under the tutelage of the great scholars of that age. Several years later, on the day of his son's return, the old man looked into the young man's eyes with great disappointment. "What have you learned, my son?" the father asked.

"I have learned everything there was to be learned, Father," he said.

"But have you learned what cannot be taught?" the father asked. "Go, my son, and learn what cannot be taught."

The young man went back to his master and asked him to teach him what cannot be taught. "Go away to the mountains with these four hundred sheep, and come back when they are one thousand," said the master.

The young man went to the mountains and became a shepherd. There, for the first time, he experienced a lasting silence, with no one to talk to but the sheep. Out of desperation, he would talk to the sheep, but they would merely look back at him as if he were stupid. Over time, he began to forget his worldly knowledge, his ego, and his pride. Ultimately, great wisdom and humility came to him.

Several years later, the small band of four hundred sheep had increased to one thousand, and the young shepherd returned to his master and fell at his feet. He had learned what cannot be taught.[1]

Throughout the history of mortal man, some of the most important lessons have been obscured by distractions. During the night of our Creator's birth, only a few wise men recognized the significance of the new star positioned over the city of Bethlehem, and only a few hillside shepherds received the glorious truths from the multitude of heavenly angels that burst forth in singing, "Glory to God in the highest."[2] Still today, the noisy and busy world in which we live would place a veil between our natural eyes and nature's important life lessons, which cannot be taught through worldly influences alone. Consequently, we fail to learn those lessons that are spiritual in nature and require something more than cerebral capacity, college degrees, and worldly experience.

Whether we realize it or not, we all live in a strange country, far from our premortal home, and we can easily become lost. Our Creator is aware of each of us. He is devoted to our daily support and care, and He provides daily direction for those who desire to receive it, not only through the trials of this life but in preparation for life after death as well. William Wordsworth (1770–1850) described our temporary residency in this mortal life as follows:

> *Our birth is but a sleep and a forgetting:*
> *The Soul that rises with us, our life's Star,*
> *Hath had elsewhere its setting,*
> *And cometh from afar:*

Not in entire forgetfulness,
And not in utter nakedness,
But trailing clouds of glory do we come
From God, who is our home:
Heaven lies about us in our infancy! [3]

All temporal and spiritual forms of life bear record of our Creator's supernal hand in the affairs of humankind. His natural creations are laid out and governed in such a way as to provide valuable lessons for those who desire His guidance in pursuing and achieving their potential. Nature is filled with lessons of life that, if followed, will lead us to a state of endless happiness and peace. By studying His physical creations that we can see, we can better understand His spiritual creations we cannot see. From this study, we can learn lessons rarely taught in the great universities of the world—lessons that are comprehended only by those subtle, quiet whisperings to the inner core of our souls. These lessons can be neither proven nor disproven by academics, who are inclined to regard such matters as foolishness and to ignore and discredit the counsels of their Creator, the great architect of the universe.

Despite this disregard, modern academics do accept various lessons that are physical in nature and that can be studied without reference to the source of their existence. For example, textbooks describe how the heavens can provide physical direction, as many land travelers and mariners from past generations have learned. During the day, due south in our northern hemisphere can be determined by the direction in which the sun is at its highest point in the sky as it slowly emerges from the east and fades away in the west.[4] For the nighttime traveler, the same can be said of movement in the sky of our moon, or any other planet or star except the North Star, which serves as a constant. The axis of our earth is pointed almost directly at the North Star and, consequently, is situated almost at the center of the wheeling circle of stars in our northern sky. Throughout the night, the North Star does not rise or set but remains very nearly in the same location all year long as the other stars circle around it.[5]

Yet many will ask, "Who needs these heavenly means of direction among today's civilized populations? Unlike the traveler of the past who relied on natural objects to find his way, who needs this method of guidance in our artificial, man-made environment? We have detailed maps, roads with well-placed signs, and even minute-by-minute computerized technology cleverly placed in our modern-day modes of transportation to guide us to our various destinations." And many will point out that the hiker and the voyager can access the sophisticated global positioning system for pinpointing their location within a few feet of virtually anywhere on earth.

The carnal mind is oblivious to the answer to this question. Those who view life solely through the prism of worldly pursuits are satisfied with achieving their temporal destinations and think they need no other. Many who receive college degrees consider themselves enlightened and self-reliant, but they fail to recognize and appreciate that they are dependent upon their Creator, who has provided not only every breath of air that sustains their mortal lives but also their very existence. In the end, their self-proclaimed wisdom barely elevates them above the intelligence of a fool, and it will profit them nothing.

Everlasting fulfillment is not achieved by relying solely on man-made light or assumed knowledge that changes with the pulse of the times. Rather than trusting in the arm of the flesh, a wise and truly educated person will look toward the heavens for a constant, as is represented by the North Star. Such guidance is reconciled with natural law and does not change with the whims of society or the vote of a board. While the sophisticated educators of today may speak with power and compelling influence, the strength of their knowledge is as small as a gnat's eyelash compared to the vastness of our Creator's power and the depth of His understanding. Furthermore, when false or deceptively inaccurate ideas are spoken by modern-day professors as truth, their teachings can be physically and morally destructive.

Truly educated people know what they must do in every situation and will align their conduct with those actions, whether they want to proceed in that direction or not. Fully educated people will know not only how to make a comfortable living but also how to maximize both immediate and eternal potential for happiness and progress. Freed from reliance upon the temporary and finite creations of man, the wise person will seek out the knowledge and light of God as the way to refinement and endless happiness. To obtain such guidance, the wise need not look far, but they must look beyond the learning of carnal man.

We are surrounded with natural forms of life that quietly encourage us in the right direction. Nature will silently say, "If ye love me, keep my commandments." She will give you a small seed that, if planted according to nature's directions, will multiply a hundredfold by means no professor is fully capable of teaching or accomplishing on his own. But nature is also disciplined. If you fail to follow her directions, she will take back that little seed and let it die. So it is with our lives. We are the agents of our own destiny and will reap what we sow.

Endotes:

1 Modarwish, (Oct. 16, 2012). "The Shepherd Story," *Muslim Academy.* Retrieved from http://muslim-academy.com/the-shepherd-story/.

2 Luke 2:14

3 Wordsworth, Ode: *Imitations of Immortality from Recollections of Early Childhood.*

4 Gooley, Tristan, (n.d.). "How to navigate using the Sun," *The National Navigator.* Retrieved from http://www.nationalnavigator.com/find-your-way-using/sun.

5 Ibid.

Lesson 2

The Side We Do Not See

There's another side to living things
   that people fail to see,
If earth had only the elements
   no life could ever be.

What makes the plants lean towards the sun
   and grow methodically?
It's not just water and dirt and light,
   it's more than chemistry.

And how can the fish, both great and small
   know when it's time to flee?
It's that part of life called consciousness
   that processes what they see.

How can the birds in the skies above
   navigate their destiny?
The spirit animates the body
   and guides them endlessly.

Mammals and reptiles breath and smell
and move majestically.
But it's more than flesh and blood and bone
that fills life's recipe.

And so with man, a mortal being
comprised miraculously,
as his spirit enters his body
his life begins to be.

As a shepherd sits on a rock while his sheep graze along a hillside, he stirs the dirt with a stick and opens the home of a little earthworm. Out of seeming curiosity, this small creature works its way out of the hole, poking its pointed head in all directions. Even though an earthworm has no eyes, the shepherd can see that the small critter is able to glean information about its surroundings through its sense of touch and its ability to perceive light.

The shepherd then asks himself, how can the educated scientists of the world claim to know so much about how life is created when they cannot even create a worm? If humans could somehow create the detailed and intricate cells that constitute the physical body of a worm and could then somehow piece them all together in their proper place, would they not still be at a loss as to how to give those cells the breath of life?

Sophisticated scientists may in turn ask, "Who is a lowly shepherd to dispute our complex laboratory experiments that demonstrate that living organisms evolve from nonliving chemicals as proof of a naturalistic origin of life?" Simple-minded people can provide a simple answer to this question. Science deals with what can be observed and reproduced through experimentation, but who created life in the first place upon which their experiments can be observed? Can anyone point to a scientist who can reproduce the nucleus of living cells, store therein significant amounts of information, and then endow those living cells with the means of processing that information? In a nutshell, what scientist can create a conscience that constitutes the spirit of a living thing? The simple answer is that, even though we appreciate what scientists are able to correctly teach us, no scientist can animate even a little worm.

Shepherds do not set out to prove or disprove anything, but this does not mean they are without personal convictions that go far deeper than fantasies of the mind. They know what their environment teaches them, lessons that are not taught at the feet of worldly professors. Nature is their school master, and it is not up to man to tell them what they know or do not know.

Naturalists commonly reject the reality of living extraterrestrial beings that cannot be seen with the physical eye, citing personal illusion, mass delusion, and "cultural viruses" as underlying causes for what they deem to be foolish beliefs. Others dismiss such beliefs as having a neurological basis, or something that the brain merely creates out of thin air as a backup defense mechanism. In 1861, a doctor named Ignaz Semmelweis pronounced an unseen link between surgeons who did not wash their hands and the high rate of infection during childbirth, but his mainstream colleagues ridiculed him in similar fashion as today's naturalists. Yet this doctor's willingness to accept something that could not be seen at that time in history led him to find the first evidence of tiny single-celled microorganisms that later became known as bacteria.[6]

As the shepherd continues to sit on the rock while his sheep graze, his dog jumps up and focuses his attention in a certain direction. There is no question in the shepherd's mind that the dog heard something his human ears could not perceive. Similarly, the shepherd knows that many animals can see things that `are beyond the perception of the human eye. Scientists claim that spiders and many insects can see a type of light called ultraviolet that most humans cannot see. They also claim that other animals, like snakes, are able to see infrared light, which means that they can see heat.[7] The shepherd concludes, "It's illogical to conclude that unless a thing can be discerned with our limited senses, such a thing cannot be real.

"So isn't it conceivable," the shepherd asks, "for a person to exist in spirit and to convey a message without the recipient physically hearing a sound or physically seeing an image? Does every communication hinge on being able to perceive through the physical senses?" The shepherd concludes, "Human beings cannot see radio waves, which carry huge amounts of information, but even I know that such waves exist, so an unseen spirit that communicates messages could likewise exist."

The shepherd then asks, "Is it a mere illusion when one undeniably senses the comforting presence of another being, accompanied by a feeling of calmness during a calamity, peace during a time of distress, or benevolence when all hope seems to have vanished?" Again he concludes that these feelings are not illusions. Shepherds, who live away from the noise and congestion of city life, find themselves in an ideal environment to take notice of such manifestations.

A shepherd does not need scientific proof to accept the existence of invisible realities. While it may not be possible to prove the existence of unseen beings through the physical senses, this does not mean that they do not exist. Belief in spiritual things generally boils down to faith, not blind or irrational faith, but faith nonetheless. As his Creator defines the word in His record, "faith is the substance of things hoped for, the evidence of things not seen."[8] In other words, faith is the assurance we can receive that a desired outcome will come to pass even though the evidence that we base that assurance upon cannot be proved through our physical senses alone. By way of example, a person exercises faith by planting a seed in the ground with the assurance, based on prior experience, that this seed will ultimately produce a beautiful, living flower. But that person cannot see what it is that gives this plant its life.

This living plant, the most beautiful of plant life's creations, leans toward the sun as it rises from the east and sets in the sky in the west. Like other forms of plant life, this flower not only embraces the light that shines, but it also depends on it to sustain life. But what differentiates a living flower from a dead one? What is it in a living plant that tells it to move in the direction of the sun?

Scientists try to explain the phenomenon in terms of a process called phototropism. They explain that plants make their food by the process of photosynthesis, whereby chlorophyll contained in a green plant's leaves converts water from the soil and carbon dioxide from the air into oxygen and sugar. The oxygen is then released into the air, and sugar is taken as food by the plant.[9] This entire process, a plant scientist will say, can only be done in the presence of sunlight, and that this necessity somehow prompts a plant to lean toward the sun. But this rather complicated analysis begs the question. That is, it merely concludes that plants lean toward the light in order to conduct photosynthesis. While scientists attempt to explain the structure of organic cells that respond to light, nothing in their analysis directly answers how plants consciously direct their physical anatomies to respond to that stimuli. Scientifically, the question remains unanswered.

Turning to animal life, what differentiates a living body from a dead one? How can a trout swimming in a quiet stream sense danger and flee as a fisherman nears its waters, or what is it within the anatomy of a hawk or a falcon that enables it to see a dying rabbit from nearly a half mile away and navigate itself through the air to feast upon its prey? What specifically is it within the cortex of a human brain that constitutes a person's conscience? The answer lies in what today's scientists still fail to fully comprehend, for it takes both a physical and a spiritual body to make and sustain life.

The shepherd recalls a stormy summer morning when he walked out on a ridge where his sheep were bedded for the night. On that rocky hilltop, he noticed the lifeless body of what otherwise appeared to be a strong and healthy sheep. He then recognized that during the night's thunderstorm, a powerful spark from the sky likely short-circuited this sheep's electrical system, causing its heart to stop. With no evidence of physical injury, he determined that this sheep did not sustain a direct strike but that perhaps she was the unfortunate recipient of the current's "choice" of a better conductor—this poor animal's body. Sufficient time had passed that there was no hope of stimulating its heart back to beating again.

The shepherd asks, "If I could somehow force this sheep's heart to pump, would it come back to life?" Generally, scientists will say that brain cells begin to die after approximately four to six minutes of no blood flow.[10] After around ten minutes, those cells will cease functioning and be effectively dead. Even though such science can be verified, the further question is, what happens to the intelligence that those living cells once hosted? Was that intelligence destroyed, or does it continue to exist outside the presence of this now-lifeless body?

Shepherds witness biological life begin and end on a regular basis. As a mother ewe gives birth to a lamb, a shepherd witnesses the breath of life enter that newborn body, a miraculous process that he knows is far deeper than our present knowledge comprehends. He understands that even if scientists are correct in saying that certain organic compounds can be created from inorganic compounds, it takes intelligence to tell that newborn physical body to get up and look for food. And he also sees from firsthand experience that when that intelligence is not present, the lifeless body will soon disintegrate into the ground.

Scientists cannot completely explain how it is that animals know when to take flight in the presence of danger. Nor can scientists thoroughly explain how animals process other information obtained from their senses. Although scientists can explain much of the chemical makeup of the nucleus of a living cell, until they understand the intelligent entities that give life to all living things, they will never be able to explain how the vast amount of information that is stored within living cells is processed.

Likewise, the humble earthbound people of the earth cannot explain the intricate processes by which our Creator formed life. They are, however, receptive to knowledge beyond that which can be perceived by empirical evidence, lessons that worldly universities do not teach.

Endnotes:

6 Semmelweis, Ignez Phillipp. (n.d.). "Dr. Semmelweis' Biography," Semmelweis Society International. Retrieved from http://semmelweis.org/about/dr-semmelweis-biography/.

7 Thompson, "How Jumping Spiders See in Color," SmartNews, Smithsonian, http://www.Smithsonianmag.com.

8 Hebrews 11:1

9 Holme, "Photosynthesis," Chemistry Encyclopedia, http://www.chemistryexplained.com.

10 Hill, "The Science and Myths Behind Lightning Strikes," https://sciencebasedlife.wordpress.com.

Lesson 3

The Universal Laws of Nature

The laws of Nature are set in place,
   without a beginning or end.
Eternal order before God's face
   these rules He did apprehend.

He found some matter in outer space
   upon which He could depend,
to make this earth for the human race
   by means humans can't comprehend.

Humans, now on Earth by heavenly grace,
   from God's love did descend.
This mortal life is now their workplace;
   on nature's law they'll depend.

No person can live so as to erase
   those rules that will never bend;
The only thing that will be displaced
   is that person the law did offend.

A shepherd quickly learns that there are certain aspects of nature that are entirely beyond his control and to which both he and his animals must conform. He easily understands the basic laws of nature. If he slips and falls down from the top of a rock ledge, he knows that he will encounter physical pain or death. He appreciates that blowing snow makes him cold and so he must put on extra clothes to stay warm and dry. He knows that if lightning begins to strike, he should remove himself from the top of a hill and seek safety in a crevice below ground level, and he likewise knows that if a forest fire starts as a consequence of a strike, he and his animals must seek safety should the fire spread out of control. Because he has no control over these aspects of his life, he must either conform with nature's laws or suffer serious consequences.

The laws of nature define the rules within which our Creator works and by which He created and populated the earth. A shepherd cannot look into the skies on a daily basis without a compelling conviction that law and order, not confusion, are the dominating principles in the universe. From the atomic realm to the vast immensity of space, it is apparent that all things are controlled, governed, and upheld by law. Nothing is arbitrary or left to chance. The same unyielding outcome will always redound from the same cause.

The laws of nature are inflexible and can be neither ignored nor changed. They constitute the rules by which planets are created and made and by which they move within their respective spheres. They are eternal, without beginning or end. They are immortal, fully immune from death's destruction. They are immutable, unyielding in principle, purpose, and application. They are irrevocable, never capable of being repealed, amended, or annulled. Finally, they are inexorable, fully incapable of being withdrawn or waived, either by persuasion or through pleading one's cause for relief.[11]

Gravity is an example of a law of nature. The law of gravity defines the degree of attraction between massive bodies. The greater the product of their masses, the greater the attraction.[12] To the shepherd, this explains why small dust particles are able to stay in the air so long and why clouds are able to hold minute water droplets before these collective tons of water start falling to the ground. If the law of gravity were suspended for even one moment, man and animals would be without control, and even our earth would physically destruct.

Matter, which can be thought of as the material or substance that human beings can readily perceive with their senses, is tied to the law of gravity and is also subject to universal law. Although Mother Nature permits matter to be altered, as for instance from a liquid to a gas, or from a solid to a liquid, according to her eternal law, matter can neither be created nor destroyed. Similarly, because matter takes up space according to universal law, the pressure of a gas under steady temperature is inversely proportional to its volume.[13]

The universal laws of nature provide a necessary consistency for progress and growth. Because man is able to foresee how the laws of nature will respond to his actions, he can focus his energies to produce a desired outcome. For example, herdsmen know that a campfire will dry their wet clothes and prevent them from getting cold. Farmers know that good seeds unfailingly bring forth fruits and vegetables of their own kind, thereby giving them confidence in producing a desirable crop to feed families across the world. Engineers apply their knowledge of a law that requires iron to expand with heat and contract with cold so they can create bridges that will not fall into rivers, cars that will not stall on roads, and airplanes that will not fall from the sky. With their understanding that water will begin to expand as it turns from a liquid to a solid at 32 degrees Fahrenheit, they can plan for such a contingency with expandable conduits and containers that will not fail with a change of weather.

But do the laws of nature also apply to things that are not made up of matter—that is, to nonphysical things? If a shepherd does not know that hard work today will bring him one step closer toward an accomplishment tomorrow, will he not his discontinue his toilsome efforts in favor of indolence and nonproductive laziness? Likewise, if integrity of character begat distrust, would that not undermine his employer's desire to enter into contractual relationships for the mutual benefit of the parties? If acts of charity begat greed, or if kindness begat harshness, would this not result in a world filled with hate and turmoil? Our Creator has ordained that every seed, material or nonmaterial, will bring forth fruit of its own kind.

Conversely, if immoral conduct did not imperil virtue, or if guilt did not torment conscience, would anyone ever be taught the value of integrity and soundness of good character? The eternal laws of our universe form the basis by which justice is assured and by which those who refuse to abide her precepts will be dammed in their ability to advance. Ultimately, these unchanging laws serve as the medium through which individuals, families, communities, and nations can chart their course, whether it be eternal happiness and progression or eternal misery and damnation.

Endnotes:

11 Muir, Leo J., *Flashes of Eternal Semaphore*, Los Angeles, California: Everett L. Sanders Company, 1928, 97.

12 Physics. (n.d.). "Sir Isaac Newton The Universal Law of Gravitation." Retrieved from htt://physics.weber.edu/amiri/physics1010online/WSUonline12w/OnLineCourseMovies/CircularMotion&Gravity/reviewofgravity/ReviewofGravity.html

13 This law is generally discussed in *Encyclopedia Britannica* under the caption Charles's Law.

Lesson 4

The Levels of Progression

Mortal man was given senses
That permit his mind to conceive
Those physical consequences
He competently can perceive.
The truths he gains, it is crystal clear.
They all begin from this lowest sphere.

Add on truths where morals belong
That our senses don't apprehend.
These are rules that spell right from wrong,
That will render a foe a friend.
Strength through justice will bring men near
The moral code of this center sphere.

The greatest truths can barely start
With books penned by imperfect men.
These are lessons felt in the heart
After prayer that ends with amen.
Spiritual truths oft met with a sneer
Are truths of this, the highest sphere.

Can it properly be said that a simple-minded, uneducated shepherd can learn important lessons beyond those which are taught in the great universities of the world? Can an innocent mind, devoid of ego and pride, receive training in the upper-division classes of the universe, where lessons are taught that are incomprehensible to the sophisticated academics of the world? Shepherds are humble people. Humility comes from the word *humus*. Even though humus is found at ground level, it is rich and fertile in its composition and character. As humus is refined organic matter, so may humble, down-to-earth people be refined by lessons others often reject.

A humble shepherd sees the earth as a marvelously planned composition of divine intelligence and wisdom, with periods of day and night, summer and winter, seed time and harvest. He feels blessed that his Creator would prepare such a magnificent system of beauty, order, and harmony for him, his family, and his fellow beings to inhabit. The earth's minerals quietly testify to him of God's systematic planning and preparation for all varieties of living things. The plant life testifies of much more than the variously colored leaves on the stalks of the flowers and the trees; they testify of deliberate planning and design. The animals that swim in the water, or that roam the earth and fly in the air, all bear witness of much more than a coincidental occurrence. "Clearly," the shepherd concludes, "I too am ever indebted to our Creator, for as His record testifies, 'In him we live, and move, and have our being.'"[14]

As he gazes into the heavens, a humble shepherd sees much more than the sun, the moon, and the stars as happenstance lamps that give warmth and light to the world; he sees perfect order, design, precision, and harmony, which are all a consequence of God's omniscient intelligence and wisdom, of His work and glory. Although his knowledge of science is limited, he looks toward the heavens and sees the majestic worlds of the universe, which include the planets (of which our earth is one), the stars (which include our sun), and our galaxy (such as our Milky Way), with everything arranged in its proper rank and order to fulfill its proper role. He then contemplates the tiniest of God's creations, the electron, the atom, and the molecule, all arranged in their proper order to fulfill the purposes for which they were designed. "Although invisible to my eye," the shepherd concludes, "these minute creations are fashioned by that same law by which the great planets of the universe came rolling into existence."

The heavens display three distinct levels of brightness between the sun, the moon, and the stars. Similarly, the lessons of nature are learned on three different gradients or dimensions of advancement: physical, moral, and spiritual. Symbolic of the lowest level of learning is the twinkling of a star, followed by a second level, which is comparable to the light of the moon, and then ultimately to the highest level of enlightenment, which may be compared to the brilliance of the sun. Symbolic comparisons aside, these three gradients of enlightenment begin first with the physical level of truth, followed by the moral level, and ultimately the spiritual.[15]

The lowest of these three gradients consists of those truths that are evident to the physical senses. The five basic senses are sight, sound, smell, taste, and touch. But our senses are deficient and incomplete, in some cases even less sophisticated than those of animals. For example, an experienced shepherd knows that if his sheep start running on a hot summer day for no apparent good cause, they probably can smell water his senses fail to recognize.

Aside from physical limitations, when our senses are functioning normally, they can become desensitized, such as with substances like alcohol or drugs. They can also become an easy target of deception. A shepherd, for example, may look toward the night sky and claim to see a halo around the moon, but in reality this is an optical illusion because the ice crystals he sees are much closer to the earth. Sensual misconceptions lead to false conclusions, and false conclusions dam progression.

People have learned to society's advantage how to amplify our senses through such tools as a telescope or a microscope. To modern-day shepherds, or "herdsmen" as they are now known, a set of binoculars has become a staple tool. Scientists use such tools to gather data and conduct experiments to enlarge their understanding of physical truths. Those truths that cannot be verified, either as apparent to the senses or via scientific proof, are often regarded as man's foolish imaginations. If, for example, laboratory experiments demonstrate that living organisms evolve naturally from nonliving chemicals, the natural man will likely see no need for a supernatural Creator whom others call God. He will then reason that if there is no God, there are no rules and no one to whom he must give an account. To the natural man, life ends at death, and during the natural struggle for life, it all boils down to survival of the fittest.

The second level of progression looks beyond this rudimentary level of establishing truth and incorporates moral truths into physical laws relating to our biological existence. These laws recognize the endowment by our Creator with certain "inalienable rights," which elevate the basic law of survival of the fittest into laws based on strength through justice, thereby resulting in a more refined state of existence. This second level of truth concentrates not only on things that are capable of perception with the physical senses but on basic differences between right and wrong. This level or sphere of truth sets forth basic rules of conduct that concentrate on such principles as justice, fair dealing, and self-restraint.

People who lack a moral foundation may not be inclined to exercise their knowledge of physical truths in society's best interest. For example, a shepherd who lacks moral decency may use his staff, not as a rod of authority to direct his sheep with loving guidance but as a means of exercising harsh brutality. Likewise, computer literate people may use their knowledge of online communication, not as a tool to advance society, but to commit fraud or identity theft. Scientists and political leaders may not apply knowledge of the physical laws of atomic power to generate heat for the common good, but for improper use of destructive bombs.

People who engage in acts of moral turpitude ignore this higher light and act out on thoughts derived entirely from the physical realm. A good indicator of whether a person has failed to advance from this lower level of learning is evidenced from his speech. Like a volcanic burst of deadly lava from a build-up of hot pressure beneath the earth's surface, an explosion of abrasive language from the mouth of the carnally minded is the mark of an insipid and ignorant soul. On the other hand, if ignorance unleashes the tongue, knowledge bridles it, just as shining a light toward a pond of frogs will bridle their persistent croaking. Someone cleverly once advanced the notion that the wise old owl would have no more wisdom than the parrot if he could talk. Among humans, whether it be in the workplace, a ball game or at home, the refined tend to be gentler in their speech. Likewise, while bombastic lectures in a classroom derive from the physical world, "the dews of heaven" are silently distilled from a higher sphere.

Like the physical realm, the moral realm of enlightenment and progression also has significant limitations. Difficulties arise in properly defining standards of moral conduct. For example, is it appropriate for a herdsman to hit a disorderly sheep, or for a parent to inflict physical pain upon an unruly child? Is the execution of a convicted murderer an immoral form of punishment? Is it morally appropriate to deny a transgender male access to female bathrooms or locker rooms? Doesn't such a denial constitute a violation of that person's civil rights? Without more enlightenment, difficult questions remain unanswered beyond a mere vote of those imperfect, yet well-meaning individuals elected to create, enforce, and adjudicate law.

There is yet a higher level of knowledge that provides guidance in answering difficult questions pertaining to standards of moral conduct, teachings that far exceed the collective capabilities of mere mortals. As the glimmer of a star is small when compared to the light of the moon in its various phases of reflection, so does the moon's light pale in comparison to the constant, undeviating brilliance of the sun. As the might makes right mentality is junior in advancement to the concept of strength through justice, so does moral enlightenment pale in comparison to spiritual knowledge, the power of righteousness. It is to this highest sphere of enlightenment that individuals, communities, and nations can draw upon as a semaphore that provides direction in overcoming the difficult issues of the day.

As darkness and evil have always been associated together, so is light associated with purity and cleanliness. At the top of the pyramid of learning and enlightenment stands our Creator, the master teacher, the Good Shepherd, who subtly reveals His truths to the humble and teachable learner who is prepared to receive: "Whom shall he teach knowledge? And whom shall he make to understand doctrine? Them that are weaned from the milk, and drawn from the breasts. For precept must be upon precept, precept on precept, line upon line, line upon line; here a little, and there a little."[16]

The proud and the profane lack the qualifications to receive these truths. They are not weaned from reliance on their physical appetites alone, or from moral rules derived by collaborative consensus of mortal minds. Enlightenment from the Good Shepherd requires the attitude of one who is humble and patient, who has replaced feelings of hate and greed with love and compassion, who seeks not only to live an honorable life but also to fully harmonize his life with the will of his Creator. Such an individual is then prepared to receive the quiet but certain guidance of the Good Shepherd and to thereby find comfort in His sheepfold.

Endnotes:

14 Acts 17:28
15 For a more detailed explanation of these levels of progression, see Ludlow, Victor L., *Principles and Practices of the Restored Gospel*, Salt Lake City, Utah: Deseret Book Company, 1992, 9–14.
16 Isaiah 28:9–10

Lesson 5

Weak-Rooted Foundations

On a cold autumn day,
      to Mother Nature's dismay,
            a woodpecker is hard at work.

The pine tree doesn't care
      that the woodpecker is there
            since the wind caused its roots to quirk.

The problem, you see,
      is that this woodpecker will be
            in a tree that can't stay alive.

Winter storms will soon peak
      with its foundation so weak,
            there's no way this tree will survive.

All this work, you'll agree,
      for this young bird's family,
            is haphazardly wrought in vain.

The wind's fierce energy
      will cause the roots to break free,
            and no birds can rightly complain.

When a man makes a house
    to shelter he and his spouse,
        he must build on a solid base.

Nature's forces won't care
    what conditions exist there
        or the dangers that he must face.

A safe home for one's soul
    will not let sin take its toll
        and commit him to agony.

God's foundation of rock
    will heaven's grand doors unlock,
        throughout all eternity.

Nature abounds with structures built by animals, such as holes for ground squirrels, hills for ants, hives for bees and wasps, elaborate nests for birds, shells for fish, webs for spiders, and dams for beavers. In addition to their architectural strength, these structures are often constructed with such sophisticated features as ventilation, temperature control, multiple escape routes, and traps.

A good example of intelligent animal architecture is the common anthill. During violent storms, these crafty little insects are safe and dry in their subterranean homes. In addition to the underground tunnels or craters they make from excavated soil, they construct hill nests called mounds made up of special kinds of materials that will absorb water and rapidly dry. Water hitting these pyramid-shaped structures tends to bead and run off the side. Even during times of heavy rain, water that enters their tunnels does not normally get very far. As an added precaution, however, ants tend to burrow at least a foot underground where they have another intricate system of tunnels that work like storm drains, allowing the water to pass without pooling.[17]

A shepherd holds a deep appreciation and sense of responsibility for our Creator's natural resources, and he is careful to avoid degradation. His sheep demonstrate a similar appreciation. If they see an anthill, they will try to avoid it and cause little if any damage as they pass by. But sometimes the unexpected happens. Despite all the planning and hard work that these little creatures exert to create a safe shelter, their well-designed place of refuge may suddenly be destroyed by unexpected forces. A large animal such as an elk, a moose, or a horse may suddenly become spooked, or a large tree may fall to the ground and destroy a colony's mound within only a few seconds.

As the shepherd contemplates this unfortunate destruction, he recognizes how remarkably little these ants know about the vastness of the world around them. Here they are, wandering around that little hill that appears no larger than a meter in diameter in this large world, with all the climates, hills, deserts, mountains, streams, rivers and oceans, and with all its various forms of vegetation and rock outcroppings, and yet this small colony of ants apprehends so very little.

And then he asks himself, "Can man begin to comprehend the unlimited expanse of space that surrounds his environment and protect himself from all potential destruction?" He realizes that, intelligent as man is, he cannot escape all possible devastating consequences on his own merits but must rely upon an intelligence and a source of power far greater than his capabilities in order to weather the various forces of destruction that could suddenly come his way.

Animals are very good at planning and preparing for anticipated events. They are good at predicting weather in the short term. A shepherd will often notice his sheep start to crowd in closer together as a storm approaches. He will see wildlife become much more active in the hours just prior to a storm. The small critters like the ants will actively cover the holes in their mounds, and the squirrels will more actively scamper about. Larger animals like deer will likewise be on the move toward more sheltered locations. Birds will hover closer to the ground as the air pressure changes, and the bees and wasps will suddenly seem to disappear.

Shepherds develop a sense of how to predict weather as well. They look into the sky and see what appears to be a halo around the sun or moon, and they conclude that a warm front will likely be followed by rain within the next twenty to twenty-four hours. Meteorologists suggest that this appearance of a halo is caused by a high cloud of ice crystals that, if they appear to form around the sun, will result in rain about 75 percent of the time, and if around the moon, about 65 percent of the time.[18]

Shepherds know that when the sun sets behind a gray sky, the western air is filled with moisture and rain is likely on its way since most weather comes from that direction. If the sky appears red in the evening hours, this is due to light passing through dust particles in the air. Because dust is associated with dry weather, the appearance of a red sky as the night approaches suggests that dry weather is coming. Conversely, if the sky appears red in the morning, he presumes that the dry air has moved away.

Experienced herdsmen take special precautions when lightning bolts begin to strike. Since they know from which direction lightning will generally pass through their location, they know that lightning activity in the north or the west requires the most precaution. They will move away from hilltops and avoid the temptation to stay dry at the base of a tree that could make a good conductor of electricity.

But what about the safety of their homes at night, when they are asleep? Herdsmen are most capable of taking care of their sheep if they spend their nights on the tops of hills where sheep instinctively prefer to bed, out of the dense mountain dew and in a less-dangerous location from predators, but also where they are more exposed to potentially lethal lightning strikes. During a lightning storm, herdsmen must be aware that lightning will generally follow the path of least resistance. Consequently, if they are in a tent, they will try to stay off the ground as much as possible and avoid contact with tent poles.

Strong winds can also cause severe damage or injury. A large tree may blow down on a tent at night, killing or severely injuring the herdsman. A simple shelter like a tent that is placed away from trees, such as on the top of a hill, must have its stakes solidly secured to the ground. It is more common for herdsmen today to live in small camps on four wheels that contain such simple amenities as a mattress and a small woodstove. If a herdsman has the luxury of a camp, he will take extra precautions by bracing large rocks against the tires to avoid the strong winds that may send his camp rolling down the hillside, possibly with him inside.

Human beings of all walks of life understand the importance of preparing for violent storms. People who live within the Great Plains tornado belt will board their windows and build storm cellars that can withstand the violent, rotating winds. Similarly, people who live in hurricane-prone areas such as along the Gulf Coast recognize the importance of not merely "toenailing" roof trusses into the top of the walls, but of securely anchoring the upper structure of their homes through the walls to the foundation. Californians and others who live in earthquake zones retrofit their homes with bolts to more firmly attach their homes to their foundations or use straps to prevent them from sliding off of their foundations.

But what if the foundation is weak? What about unexpected events for which they did not plan and carefully prepare, such as an unanticipated flood? Regardless of where a home is constructed, architects and builders know that the stability of a building is dependent on the depth, strength, and integrity of its foundation, sufficient to support the weight of their homes upon the various types of ground.

These lessons people have learned to protect themselves and their homes from violent storms address only the physical aspects of life. There are also vitally important lessons that are elevated from the physical to the moral or even the spiritual levels of our lives. The consequences of a weak moral foundation in one's home can be just as devastating to its inhabitants as a weak physical foundation, the only difference being the level or dimension of existence.

It is no secret that marriages that are built on an immoral foundation of infidelity and cruelty are frequently dissolved and families are broken. Conversely, families that are rooted with deep convictions of marital trust, loyalty, and family unity are far less likely to succumb to the violent storms that so often surround separation, divorce, and child custody disputes.

Fewer people recognize the importance of building marital relationships and raising their children on strong spiritual foundations. People can see the consequences of homes that are constructed on weak moral foundations, but their views of eternal consequences are not open to public view and require faith in the words of their Creator. While strong moral foundations promote continuity and family togetherness during life, strong spiritual foundations withstand the devastating effects of death and pave the way for relationships to continue beyond the grave.

In laying out the basic requirements of a sound spiritual foundation, our Creator's record provides: "Therefore whosoever heareth these sayings of mine, and doeth them, I will liken him unto a wise man, which built his house upon a rock: And the rain descended, and the floods came, and the winds blew, and beat upon that house; and it fell not: for it was founded upon a rock."[19] The rock to which our Creator was referring was Himself, who set the perfect example of how to temper anger, discipline thoughts, maintain integrity, and prioritize family and fellow citizens over worldly riches.

Even the casual observer of God's creations will notice that His works are based upon principles of obedience and order. The word *order* has reference to "a rank, a row, or a series." Related to *order* is the word *ordain,* which refers to the process by which things are called into order, and the word *ordinance,* which refers to the ceremony or formality applied to memorialize entry into a specific set of laws or commands. As pertaining to human beings, these ordinances or ceremonies allow the participant to agree by covenant to obey such laws, the violation of which results in punishment. People with a strong spiritual foundation recognize the importance of entering into solemn covenants with their Creator to abide by His laws, thereby committing formally to create a solid foundation that can withstand the storms of life.

The integrity of a strong spiritual foundation will not only enable us to endure the mighty storms that otherwise drag people down to misery and endless regret during this life, but it will also provide an open door for eternal salvation and endless happiness when this brief mortal life ends.

Endnotes:

17 Prabhakar, Dektar & Gordon, "How does an ant colony coordinate its behavior?" *Public Library of Science Journal,* August 28, 2012.

18 Kershner, (n.d.). "Does a ring around the moon mean rain is coming soon?" *Science.* Retrieved from http://science.howstuffworks.com/nature/climate-weather/atmospheric/ring-around-the-moon-mean-rain-is-coming-soon.htm.

19 Matthew 7:24–25

Lesson 6

Struggle Begets Strength

A plant born in a gravel pit
  needs a struggle to survive.
This world just doesn't care a bit
  if it dies or stays alive.

A seed that doesn't recommit
  when nature's troubles arrive,
will find itself inadequate
  for its vigor to revive.

Since plants that struggle do permit
  natural strength and inner drive,
the bottom line of all of it
  is that conflict helps them thrive.

As larvae in cocoons transmit
  liquid that their wings derive,
hard work and the cocoon will split
  same as bees in a beehive.

The man who's just about to quit
    has to buckle down with drive,
to nature's laws he must submit
    at least to age sixty-five.

So muscle, nerve and grit befit
    all those men who will arrive,
Exalted up on high to sit
    where no blessings are deprived.

At times a shepherd returns to his tent or camp wagon late in the evening, wet and cold. The storm continues through the night, with no sign of letting up. He crawls out of bed before the break of dawn and puts on his stiff, damp trousers in preparation for another day, but the cold is no deterrent because the nerve and grit he has developed over the years have made him that way. He knows from experience that the rain will pass, and nature has taught him that if he is ever to see the rainbow, he must endure the storm.

From the first breath of his life, that same energy that was necessary to exit his mother's womb passes on through to him, a source of strength upon which he can draw to overcome the impending trials that await in his life ahead. As he listens carefully, he will be able to hear those same voices of encouragement that were given to his exhausted mother— push, push, push! His mother cries out in pain, but she pushes on. In a short time, her pain is shared and then passed on to him as a mortal individual, unwelcome feelings that he must now claim as his own, feelings of stress, loneliness, anxiety, sorrow, and pain that will return again and again throughout the remainder of his years. But he presses on because he knows the dark storms of his life will pass and will leave him in a stronger position to endure the next trial to come.

From struggle, strength is born, not only among human beings but in all varieties of nature. In the mineral kingdom, we find that a diamond, the most precious of all stones, is coal made good under pressure. Gold, a precious metal, goes through the "refiner's fire," an intense heat that is created to burn out all the impurities and dross. And when the furnace has been sufficiently endured, all that remains of the ore is the gold itself, pure and beautiful. The shepherd recalls being told that our Creator uses processes comparable to a refiner's fire by which He will try His people and purge them as gold.[20]

This principle is written into every chapter of biological life. In the plant kingdom, the shepherd observes that plants struggle to grow and remain alive. Grass competes for sunlight to grow in the sagebrush stands because brush dominates in the fight for light and moisture, and even trees struggle with each other as they compete for these necessary components of life.

Insects struggle. A butterfly is incapable of flight until it has struggled sufficiently to free itself from the cocoon, giving its wings the strength to fly in the process. Insects compete with insects, feeding on each other or other forms of life. Brute beasts also struggle. Despite their physical strength, organisms as small as bacteria will seek to consume their massive bodies from within. Meanwhile, the birds, reptiles, and all other varieties of animal life must struggle to stay alive. The supreme reward of all this struggle is strength. Muscle, nerve, grit, wisdom, and integrity of body and mind are all products of adversity and taken as a whole, constitute character. The hardest a man will ever struggle defines how strong he will ever be.[21]

A shepherd knows that he is not alone during times of difficulty. He may not have the immediate convenience of family or friends to offer encouragement, but his surroundings provide all the support he needs. As he rides to his sheep on his sure-footed horse during a cold and wintery morning, he is amazed that despite the impressive power of this twelve hundred–pound gelding to do as he pleases, the horse loyally works his way through the snow to the top of the hill, carefully transporting the chilled and weary body of his master on his strong back. The work dogs follow closely behind, caked with snow but eager to lend their moral support. The trail progresses upward through a grove of dormant, barren trees, having already stored sufficient energy to get them through the winter. Most assuredly, the herdsman relies on the tender mercies of his Creator to bridge his weaknesses, to calm his fears, and to renew his confidence as he passes through another array of life's challenges.

What does his Creator tell him? As this cold herdsman leaves the grove of trees, he observes a large, ragged old tree standing all alone in the cold winter wind. He recognizes that this tree is like a lonely person, not like a weak beggar, but like a great prominent man who has withstood the tests of time despite the lack of a family at his side to lend support. Above the ground, while its branches fight for stability in the wind, its roots rest unshaken, as if to say to the world, "You can shake my limbs and even break a branch of mine or two, but my roots have grown ever stronger since my birth. You'll never touch them, for they are the deepest part of me." That great tree silently goes on to say, "If you cut me down, the sun will shine down on my open wound and reveal to the world each year of my life that I have struggled through the winds, the droughts, the fires, the pestilence, the solitude, and the loneliness." This tree trunk, the herdsman concludes, will have the narrowest of rings, the hardest of wood, having grown high in the mountains where the destructive forces of nature demand the greatest struggle.

This herdsman is reminded of his own roots, not only of the sacrifices and trials of his mortal ancestry but of those uncertain roots that predated his mortal birth. He then contemplates how the strength of his character may be described when he achieves the age of a tree.

Although he recognizes that his capacity for physical strength may decrease with the passage of time, he knows that his mental integrity will only strengthen as he weathers the storms.

Nature teaches this young man that while mortal life in this sphere of existence was never intended to be easy, the product of adversity is integrity and character. He recognizes that every conflict he subdues today will only increase his confidence to face his trials tomorrow. He appreciates that the blessing of courage comes from challenges, and the blessing of wisdom comes from pain and deep wounds. In short, he has connected that vital link between the two great conflicts of nature: the external struggle from the outside world versus the internal struggle it takes to cope with life's challenges. Having welded these two conflicts firmly together, the strength of his soul is placed within his clear vison with each passing challenge that he overcomes.

In the end, it will be known among all people that our Creator allows adversity into our lives not to break us but to better us, to enable us to grow in strength physically, mentally, socially, and spiritually. Our Creator allows adversity because He knows that the most refined people are those who have experienced loneliness, defeat, suffering, and misery and who have found their way out of the depths of despair. Having successfully overcome these trials, these are the people who are sensitive to others who struggle, who are filled with compassion, kindness, and love. These qualities are not freely bestowed but are a product of the experiences of mortal life.

Endnotes:

20 See Malachi 3:2–3.
21 Muir, Leo J., *Flashes of Eternal Semaphore*, Los Angeles, California: Everett L. Sanders Company, 1928, 15–16.

Lesson 7

Shortcuts

A shortcut is a quicker way
    to a desired end,
But nature says we must obey
    a rigid discipline.

We take shortcuts when we travel
    but do we comprehend?
Back roads often turn to gravel,
    far better not to begin.

Quitting school for a simple job
    to buy a brand new car,
may one day cause our heads to throb
    and progress it will bar.

And pills to improve appearance
    to discard exercise,
can't replace the perseverance
    so pleasing to the eyes.

Some claim they like to gamble
and pursue easy wealth,
but hard work is the preamble
for better mental health.

There are those who value fashion
as a social reward,
but character as a passion
augments the spinal cord.

Nature provides the right answer
to reach our destiny,
while shortcuts are like a cancer
they're nature's penalty.

On a sunny June day along a mountain road in southern Idaho, a couple driving a luxurious car became lost and sought directions from a herdsman who was tending a band of sheep. "How do you get to Nevada?" the elderly driver asked. In one of his hands was a map on which he had marked his route, but ambiguous road signs caused confusion. He indicated that he and his wife had set out to see the beautiful mountain landscape on a route they had chosen which, they thought, would take far fewer miles to reach their destination. They were troubled that the dirt road had become rough and somewhat rutted, but they seemed determined to continue along their chosen course.

Reluctantly, the herdsman informed the couple that the road they had chosen was still covered with a massive snow drift located over a pass several miles ahead. The couple's only recourse was to go back to where they had started and take the long road around the mountain. Mother Nature would not allow them to take this attractive shortcut that seemed at the time to be the easiest and most pleasant way to reach their destination.

The herdsman reminds himself that many people court a myopic view of the laws that nature requires of them, always looking for a shortcut. They search for shorter, quicker, or easier ways to get to a certain place or to fulfill a desired end. Often, he is reminded, mistakes are made or frustrations are encountered when shortcuts are taken. Nature teaches that the easiest or less demanding way does not generally produce the desired result.

The herdsman then reflects on other types of shortcuts that can adversely affect people's lives. He looks at his own life and wonders if there is not some means of doing better. He asks himself, "Could I ever drive a luxurious car like that couple was driving?" He ponders what other people his age might be doing to live fulfilled and successful lives as he, alone and far from family and friends, watches his sheep graze.

He is reminded of a friend, a competent young man who had the means that he never had to progress in school but decided to short-circuit this more secure road to success by leaving school for a mediocre job. "Why do I need a better education?" his friend asked. "Am I less competent than the lowly spider who knows instinctively how to create a web? Aren't the predators like the coyote and the bear naturally born hunters? And don't birds and wasps know how to build nests without being taught?" Despite his correct observations, he failed to recognize that animals also develop learned behaviors to protect and enhance their lives. Spiders learn how to capture insects. Predators learn how to hunt from their mothers, and the older, more experienced birds do a better job building nests. He failed to appreciate that the more a person learns how to improve or prolong his life and the lives of others, the more fulfilled his life will be.

He imagines further that as his friend grows older, he might become dissatisfied with his physical appearance. As has been Mother Nature's call from the earliest of mortal man's existence, she screams, "Run for your life!" But rather than obeying her call, this man seeks out the quickest or the easiest way to improve his appearance, rejecting nature's way, which requires a pattern of rigorous work or exercise in favor of diet pills to help him lose weight or steroids to enlarge his muscle mass. While his shortcut to improved physical appearance may give him his desired reduced weight or "macho" physique, his vital organs are deprived of needed exercise and become weak and sickly. In the end, his goal of improved physical appearance becomes frustrated and compromised.

As midlife approaches, this same man has a family and recognizes a need to enhance is income beyond that which he receives from his low-hour, minimum-wage job. Rather than exerting effort to improve his skills or to take on a second job, he decides to try his luck by purchasing lottery tickets or entering into other games of chance. Mathematical statistics prove correct, and his anxiety increases with each unlucky draw. Even worse, he falls to nature's trap of idle time, the so-called devil's workshop.

Nature teaches that animals that spend much of their day foraging for food are more likely to use their additional time resting rather than on exercising aggressive behavior. Sheep, for example, are known for their mild and temperate dispositions. They follow a diurnal pattern of activity, feeding from dawn to dusk and stopping sporadically to rest and chew their cud. On the other hand, nature's extremely efficient predators, such as the cougar, the bear, or the python, seem to have much more free time. Likewise, men with idle time seem more prone in society to be given that loathsome name of predator than is the case of the industrious, hardworking individual.

Referring back to this young man who had filled his life with shortcuts, his hair has now grown gray with the passage of time. His life's decisions have molded his character and now clearly define the man he has become at his very core. He looks back on his life and sees a rather unsophisticated individual who took shortcuts throughout his life, even on decisions that affected his physical health. But true to form, he still chooses man's way over nature's way. Rather than improving his appearance from within, he focuses on his outside appearance. He dyes his hair back to its original color, purchases attractive clothing, and places a gold chain around his neck. But once again, his shortcuts in life leave him unfulfilled and disappointed.

In time, this same man will die. Although his earthly remains will decompose back into Mother Earth, that portion of his soul that gave his body the breath of life when he entered this world will live on, as will also those eternal laws of nature. As in mortal life, these immutable laws provide no shortcuts to salvation. That same person who inhabited his mortal body will take that same undisciplined character to the spirit world. In the end, he will find that there are no shortcuts to heaven.

The herdsman concludes that perhaps his job is not so bad. He recognizes that although he is not wealthy in terms of material riches, he is able to provide for the needs of his family in the way that his Creator has designed. He is on a road that leads him to being physically fit, morally straight, and mentally sharp. His conscience is clear of regrets, and his life is free of the pride and vanity of the world. In short, he says, "I am taking the more difficult path that allows me to fill the measure of my creation."

Lesson 8

Why the Sky Is Blue

From a scientific view, when we look into the sky
        we behold a sea of blue, which the sunlight's rays supply.
Air born dust emits this hue, when its wavelengths reach our eye,
        somewhat difficult but true, it's an atmospheric dye.

Theologians see this blue, when we look into the sky
        symbolically heaven's clue, of the color of God's eye.
For He sees all that we do, and no deeds will pass Him by
        he discerns us through and through, from our birth until we die.

Whether atheist or Jew, Christian or some other guy,
        every morning right on cue, from the east we can rely
as the moon bids its adieu, the sun comes rising high
        as a sign to me and you, of new life after we die.

So no matter what we do, it's important that we try
        diligently to be true, and to every rule comply.
There's no need to sit and stew, and no need to moan and sigh
        God can all darkness subdue, as His blue skies testify.

As a shepherd passes time while his sheep graze a hillside, he observes the light blue sky and ponders the thought that aside from the sky and the sea, the color blue doesn't appear much in nature. Blue rocks are rare, the animal kingdom is nearly barren of the color blue except for a few eyes, and with the exception of a few flowers, blue plant life is scarce.

The shepherd concludes, "What better color than blue could our Creator have given the sky and the sea to give variety and beauty to the earth?" This is a color, he believes, that stands for open, expansive spaces and limitless freedom of thought, inspiration, and intuition. The soft blue sky adds much to calm his tensions and aid his concentration. To him, it seems to be the color of clear, uninhibited, and never-ending communication with heaven and earth.

The shepherd then ponders, "How might such a communication to or from the heavens work?" Thanks to scientists, he appreciates that energy is transmitted through space in waves, such as sound waves or light waves. Sound waves require a medium, or something to travel through, such as air, water, glass, or metal. Sound waves that travel through a dense medium, such as hardened steel as opposed to a liquid or a gas, will carry at a much faster speed and also at a much greater distance than is the case of a less-dense medium, such as air. Regardless of the medium used, friction will cause the vibrations of sound waves to become quieter and quieter until they completely fade away.[22]

A light wave, on the other hand, does not require a medium to pass from a definite point source (such as from a light bulb or a star) as is the case of a sound wave originating from a source such as an instrument, an animal, or a noisy machine. Further, since a light wave can travel through empty space without interacting with anything else, it will not dissipate or grow smaller, no matter how far it travels. Additionally, a light wave travels electromagnetically and does not require the alternate compression and expansion of matter, and for this reason, it also travels much faster than a sound wave. A light wave can travel through air and empty space at an amazing speed of 186,000 miles per second, whereas a sound wave traveling through air as a medium must travel at a much slower speed of approximately 1,100 feet per second.[23]

The shepherd wonders, "Can I learn to hear sounds of a different wavelength or frequency that my physical ears cannot presently perceive without assistance?" And then he wonders, "Can I comprehend communications sent through light waves? Can I see things that my physical eyes cannot see, or can I feel things that my physical body is unable to feel? In short," he asks himself, "do I have spiritual sensitivities with which I can hear or see or feel, which are separate and distinct from my physical senses?"

Light can be divided into two types, physical and spiritual. There is a relationship between the physical light that emanates from the sun and spiritual light that emanates from our Creator. Light dispels darkness in both instances. When physical or spiritual light is present, darkness is vanquished and must depart. Light and darkness cannot occupy the same space at the same time, for as light increases, darkness is dispelled proportionally.

In the physical world, the sun is the source of all our physical energy, whether in the form of heat or light. Plants require sunlight to make food in a process called photosynthesis. Likewise, animals require sunlight for food. Even nocturnal animals (night animals) require light because they feed on living things that receive their energy from the sun. While the majority of the sunlight falling on Earth is not captured by plants, it becomes heat, which is also necessary for all plant and animal life.

As physical light is necessary for the physical well-being of a person's physical body, spiritual light is necessary to sustain spiritual health. Insufficient spiritual light will either slow or entirely stop the progress of a living soul, even to the point where that soul is considered spiritually dead until such time as spiritual light can once again be received.

As the light of the sun enters the body through a human's natural eyes, so the light of heaven can illuminate a person's soul through his or her spiritual eyes. Through the use of both physical light and spiritual light, humans can find their way, not only through the dark paths of physical life but through spiritual darkness as well. Through these means, a person's body can ultimately become filled with light to the extent that there is no darkness in him or her and he or she is able to see and comprehend all things, both physical and spiritual.

Some may ask if spiritual nourishment and enlightenment are freely given to all who seek such illumination. Regarding His physical creations, when our Creator sees a giant tree or a small blade of grass yearn for water, He sends a cloud in His own time that brings rain on everything within its reach regardless of size, age, or species. Mother Nature does not discriminate among her creations but invites all to freely partake of her life-giving moisture. And once the thirst is quenched, He sends the light of the sun to shine upon all of nature's creations regardless of their strength or status.

Our Creator is no less discriminatory with His spiritual light. Symbolically speaking, as the thirsty and choking shepherd in a desert is provided a natural spring to quench his thirst and to find an escape from an agonizing death, all weary travelers wandering through the trials of mortality are freely offered His ever-present spring of "living water," which, if sought and accepted, leads to peace in this life and unending happiness in the life to come. Of course, the shepherd knows where to look to find the spring that will quench his thirst, and he must expend effort to place himself at that source. This is no less true with quenching one's spiritual thirst. While spiritual enlightenment and knowledge are freely extended to everyone, it can come only by expending energy to place oneself at the proper source and then partake of its goodness.

For centuries shepherds have been regarded by many as unclean and socially undesirable. But are these humble, simple, and straightforward people unclean or otherwise so unrefined in the eyes of their Creator as to render them unworthy of His favor? The answer is an unequivocal no. Moses was a shepherd when God appeared to him at the burning bush on one of nature's natural temples referred to as "the mountain of God."[24] The great king David was a shepherd boy who was not chosen by man's standards according to God's record, "for man looketh upon the outward appearance, but the Lord looketh upon the heart."[25]

Out of the blue, several questions come to the shepherd's mind. "If our Creator knew the hearts of people in times of old, does reason not also suggest that He can also see into the hearts of men living today? Can my Creator also see into my heart? And if He sees that my intent is good, will He not also freely give me His spiritual light?"

"Can my Creator look down on me at this very hour?" the shepherd asks. "Can He likewise look down upon individuals throughout this world and see all that is good and bad, happy or miserable, comfortable or stressed, healthy or in search of succor and strength? Of course He can," the shepherd concludes. If man is given the opportunity from his Creator to freely receive light to see and understand the good and bad in all things, would not our Creator also freely reserve unto Himself the ability to look down on His creations and see all the honorable and praiseworthy, and all the dark and lonely paths that man traverses? And assuming that our Creator is vested with such knowledge, does it not also follow that

He would be in a position to provide loving direction and guidance to all who desire to receive it? Without any hesitancy, the shepherd concludes with a profound yes to each of these questions.

The shepherd then moves on to another thought. While the sun comes up every morning as a reminder to all humankind that renewed life is freely given to all of God's creatures regardless of their physical or spiritual state, the shepherd contemplates that the lessons of nature also suggest that the sun's gentle rays will participate in the replication of whatever type of seed is planted. Likewise, a man's character is the product of the thoughts, words, and actions that he plants in his mind and in his heart. Our Creator is aware of each of His creations and will reward them with a new life of like kind, be it desirable or undesirable, just as a dead plant will spring up the following season with a virtual replicant of itself. Man is given the agency to create the character of his own soul. Nature's lessons remind people everywhere that every action has consequences and that all their deeds, be they good or evil, will be accompanied with a resulting blessing or punishment.

In our civilized society, the color blue also symbolizes authority and force. A police officer, dressed in a blue uniform, enforces those laws that society has set in place. He patrols the streets in search of those who fail to abide by the law, and if he sees a violator, he flashes his blue lights and executes the law that fits the nature of the infraction or crime. Similarly, our Creator, vested with power and authority, sees all that we do and justly executes His eternal laws according to the good or evil that He sees in our behavior.

As the day proceeds, the shepherd turns his attention to a choir of lambs bleating for their mothers, and he admires how a mother ewe is able to readily discern the individual sound of her lamb among all the hundreds of others who are bleating at the same time. He then recognizes that sometimes people conscientiously hear only those sounds that they are listening for, like a ball player in the middle of a game who is able to discern the sound of his mother's voice urging him on while, at the same time, he subconsciously blocks out a host of other vociferous fans, or like a mother who wakes to the sound of her baby's cry while the rest of the family sleeps on. He recalls hearing a story told of a man in a crowded park who was impressed with the magnificent sound of the birds singing in the trees.[26] When no one else seemed to hear this pleasing sound, the man reached into his pocket and pulled out a coin. When he flung it into the air, the coin hit the cement pavement with a distinct ring, no louder than the signing of the birds. Everyone impulsively looked in the direction of the sound of the coin. We hear what we train our minds to hear.

With the darkening sky, the shepherd begins to feel left alone. To some degree, he longs for that lost light as he fumbles his way around in the darkness. He thinks again to himself, *Under the light blue sky everything about me was in plain view, but now everything seems secretive and hidden.* He has only himself, his animals, and nature with which to deal, and for him an air of mystery hides behind every tree in the dark of night.

Should he be unable to return to camp as the dark sky arrives, he knows that he can create his own little temple of light with the small blaze of a fire to give him comfort and warmth. He knows that a small fire will also give predators cause to maintain their distance. But despite the darkness of night, he knows that his heart is right before his Creator and that the armor of light that penetrates every fiber of his soul will see him through the night. The shepherd's mood is uplifted, and he can pass the night more peacefully. And with the passing of every night, the rising sun will once again bring new light and life.

Endnotes:

22 Grolier Incorporated (1993). "Acoustics." In *Encyclopedia Americana* (111–13). Danbury, Connecticut.

23 Grolier Incorporated (1993). "Electromagnetic Radiation." In *Encyclopedia Americana* (156–62). Danbury, Connecticut.

24 Exodus 3:1

25 1 Samuel 16:7

26 McConkie, Joseph Fielding, referencing Packer, Boyd K. in *The Spirit of Revelation*, Salt Lake City, Utah: Deseret Book, 1984, 65.

Lesson 9

The Sun Will Shine Again

When clouds grow dark and fog sets in
    God's creations seem unkind
Nature follows a discipline
    that all living things must mind.

Bleak days bring moisture where within
    plants and animals can find,
life's blood that could have never been
    if just sunshine were designed.

Times grow tough and to our chagrin
    confidence is undermined;
gird up your loins, lift up your chin,
    take faith in the Mastermind.

Darkness in death, turmoil and sin
    can render us unaligned;
but God can make it shine again
    He'll light a path for the blind.

When a shepherd pitches his tent or places his sheep wagon (typically called a "camp") for the night, it is common to face the door toward the east. There are likely many reasons for this tradition, one of which is to protect the doorway from the winds and rains that regularly come from the west. Indian tribes in North America were known to situate the doorways of their teepees or "hogans" facing east to welcome the rising sun for good wealth and fortune.[27] Likewise, it is customary for Christian people to bury their dead with their feet pointed eastward, traditionally for the reason that the dead may symbolically look in the direction from where their Savior will return "like the rising sun" to raise them to life.[28]

The sun renews life on a daily basis, a regular reminder from our Creator that He will not only sustain life in mortality but also that His dead will rise again. The sun not only renews life but also serves as our source of light and direction. Our Creator sends the sun's rays across ninety-three million miles of cold, dead space and then releases their warmth for our benefit only when they strike our atmosphere.

On a foggy, cold morning in the hills of southern Idaho, a herdsman is out with his sheep when his boss approaches his camp with groceries. Desiring assurance that his herdsman is content, the employer listens in the fog for the ringing bells on the necks of some of his sheep in order to determine his location. Upon hearing the deep ring of a bell in the far distance, he drives his pickup truck as close to the sound of the bell as the brushy terrain will allow and then proceeds through the snow and foggy terrain on foot. Finding his herdsman in good spirits, he starts back toward his vehicle, but he cannot find it. He is lost in the fog.

For hours the employer searches for his pickup truck, even at times crossing over his own foot tracks, but his search is in vain. Finally, as the sun begins to shine through the dense fog, he is able to see the way back to his desired location. Upon returning to camp, he finds his herdsman in the warmth and comfort of his shelter.

"How did you return to camp so quickly?" his employer asks.

The herdsman replies, "Oh, it was easy. My horse knows the location of his oats, so I simply hopped on his back and gave him the reins!"

The herdsman taught his employer an important lesson. When we become lost in this bleak and lonely world, we are never without assurance that our circumstances will improve as we endure the present and faithfully place our trust in the superior knowledge and care of the good grace of someone or something besides our own limited understanding. While a horse's judgment is imperfect despite its best intent, our Creator will not let us down as we seek His guidance on those occasions when there appears to be no place to turn for direction. There will come those times when we simply must give our Creator the reins and place our trust in Him that He will lead us back home to comfort.

Speaking of our Creator's care, an account is given in His record of the young servant of a prophet named Elisha who cried out as he and his people were surrounded by enemies, "Alas, [what] shall we do?" Elisha answered, "Fear not: for they that be with us are more than they that be with them." Then Elisha prayed, "Lord, … open his eyes, that he may see." And the Lord did open the eyes of the young man, and he did see that the mountain was full of horses and chariots of fire round about Elisha .[29]

A shepherd, when fearful or depressed, may ask, "What shall I do?" In fear he gasps for a breath of air, and his question is suddenly answered. He cannot see the oxygen that gives him life, nor can he see the force of gravity that keeps his feet on the ground. But if he asks his Creator in faith, his spiritual eyes will open, and he will be able to see with his spiritual eyes and hear with his spiritual ears those subtle but sure assurances from the unseen world.

Everyone knows that stressful and gloomy days accompany mortal life. They come and go regardless of every effort to avoid them. A shepherd may receive a message from his foreign home that an earthquake has killed hundreds of innocent victims, or that his daughter has been severely injured in an accident, or that his wife has lost a courageous battle with cancer. He may fear for the well-being of his son, a college student in a large city and all alone, who questions the value of his life as daily challenges choke his hope for a positive ending.

"Are these tragedies that have hurt my innocent family and friends fair?" the shepherd asks. "Would a just God permit innocent people to suffer such afflictions? In a universe that is engineered with perfect precision, would our perfect Creator deliberately allow such horrific things to happen?" At a moment of desperation at his inability to provide immediate consolation and relief, the shepherd looks to his Creator and asks, "Why me?" as if He had looked down on this lonely and distressed soul and dispersed these terrible deeds without provocation.

And then, from nowhere, a subtle reminder quietly distills upon his understanding. This is a world where corruption is allowed to exist, where sorrow and pain are ever present, and where inequity and unfairness are a reality of mortal life. Seeking fairness in this world of corruption is like searching for the stars on a cloudy night; though they are there, you cannot find them. But in the end, this shepherd is assured, the skies will clear and the sun will always return.

The bewildered shepherd then recognizes that his Creator could have reserved to Himself all power to control his life, shielding him and his loved ones from every type of calamity. Through His almighty power and His perfect knowledge and wisdom, He could have created the planet Earth so as to spare man from every type of heartache, grief and pain, and even from death and decay.[30] The book of Genesis in His holy record describes such a creation. "So what happened," the shepherd asks, "to bring us to the bleak circumstances that I now encounter, where I must witness the misery, sickness, pain, and death of my loved ones?"

The answer now seems clear: "You were created in an environment whereby you could learn and grow." His Creator explains, "I created a place where you could experience what it's like to feel pain in order that you may fully appreciate comfort, where sorrow and misery may be understood in order that you may appreciate joy and happiness, and even where one day you will experience mortal death as a pathway to renewed and fulfilled life, just as a seed decays in the ground so it may spring up into a more glorious state of existence."

The shepherd then understands. "To shield me from all my sorrow and suffering would prevent me from learning how to cope with and ultimately overcome life's challenges and difficulties. If I were to view the entirety of my existence within the perimeters of my mortal existence, then all the pain, sorrow, and stress of my life clearly would be a calamity, but such is not the case."[31]

"I do not view your life merely as a momentary snap shot in time as you do," his Creator says. "I do not look down upon you and see your life according to your limited understanding, but from a far different perspective, from your primal beginning, which stretches far back into your pre-earth past and extending far into the distant eternities beyond this life." Indeed, as Wordsworth penned, our birth is but a sleep and a forgetting, and heaven truly does lie about us in our infancy!

The shepherd learned on this difficult day one of the great lessons of nature. In keeping with the universal laws of nature, Mother Nature's provision for physical light is symbolic of man's access to spiritual light.

She teaches that when we are lost physically, we can rely upon her physical light, but if we become lost spiritually we can, through faith, obtain spiritual light and knowledge. As our Creator's sacred record provides, "I am the light of the world: he that followeth me shall not walk in darkness, but shall have the light of life."[32]

With the wakening of each new day, the sun returns again, not only with life-giving light, which is showered equally upon all men regardless of their physical or moral status before Him, but with a sense of renewed warmth and hope that offers a fresh start on a new day. No doubt the sun comes up each morning and shines down on all life in its present state, be it good, bad, or indifferent, but each new day it reminds us that the rigors of today need not remain in status quo for a new tomorrow. As with the light of the sun, the spiritual "light of life" is free for all who follow our Creator's counsel and seek His guiding light.

Endnotes:

27 Long, Clayton (n.d.). "Navajo Homes—Hogans." Retrieved from http://navajopeople.org/navajo-hogans.htm.

28 See for example a story out of Ceredigion, West Wales, where a number of elderly residents approached the Ceredigion council to rectify the problem of bodies being buried the wrong way in their town cemetery, north to south instead of east to west. BBC (Feb. 23, 2012). Retrieved from http://www.bbc.com/news/uk-wales-mid-wales-17140489.

29 2 Kings 6:15–17

30 This thought is more thoroughly presented by Kimball, Spencer W., *Tragedy or Destiny*, Salt Lake City, Utah: Deseret Book Co., 1977, 1–12.

31 Ibid.

32 John 8:12.

Lesson 10

The Fate of a Mighty Tree

The largest pine in a forest
became the weakest and poorest
because it happened to be
an unlucky host of a wee,
small beetle the size of a pea.

The test for this mighty tree
as one could easily see
was no grand emergency
but what subtly came to be
a pest that kills by degree.
        Any man with vision could see
        that life was lost tragically.

The strongest man in a town
bruised his soul without a frown
by a sin which came to be
a habit he failed to see
that spoiled his integrity.

This man's test was not to be
a sin the size of a tree
but one that most certainly
would stymie his energy
and kill his soul by degree.

A strong man brought to his knee,
his life was a tragedy.

A primary goal of a shepherd is to provide his animals with the best available food and water. Other things he and his animals will require to sustain life but that seem to be provided in abundance include air, sunlight, and a temperature that is neither too hot nor too cold. If life only required a shepherd to concentrate on these five essential things, his job would be free of many obstacles and trials. Unfortunately, this is not the case.

There are other limiting factors that are placed in his way. Aside from too much or too little of any of those things mentioned above, there are other challenges that pose significant or even life-threatening difficulty, including disease-carrying agents, predators, poisonous plants, and certain physical barriers, such as large patches of down timber or rock ledges. If these obstacles are not carefully watched for and prevented, serious illness, injury, or even death may result.

Mother Nature teaches her occupants to constantly be on guard against physical injury or destruction. All forms of life, whether it be in the plant kingdom or the animal kingdom, must defend themselves against both anticipated and unanticipated threats and aggression. Unfortunately, attention is often centered upon anticipated immediate or severe threats, with little attention given to the seemingly insignificant forces that can gradually result in complete destruction.

Plants instinctively learn to protect themselves from becoming someone's or something's dinner. They may grow defense mechanisms such as thorns, toxic oils, repugnant smells, or thick skins. Cactus plants, for example, grow thorns to protect themselves against being trampled on or eaten. Other plants may develop repulsive scents that animals find distasteful, or they may create thick skins or oils that are poisonous if eaten.

Herdsmen in the Rocky Mountains are careful to watch for toxic plants, such as a small plant called halogeton that grows in arid deserts and can kill sheep within hours if eaten. Other plants, like stinging nettles, which naturally grow in the higher elevations, would likely have been eliminated years ago from the many insects and animals eating this otherwise very healthy plant, had it not been for its so-called stinging hairs, which are little hollow tubes with walls of silica making them into tiny glass needles.[33]

But despite these defensive means plants have developed to protect against aggression, what about those subtle, surreptitious invasions that start out as relatively harmless but that if unchecked, will ultimately choke the life of its host? Many plants, such as stinging nettles, defend themselves against insects, but other forms of plant life do not seem to pay much attention to the little critters. Mother Nature offers help to protect plant life from these discrete invasions of insects, providing disease-causing organisms like viruses, bacteria, protozoa, fungi, and nematodes, but even these enemies of insects can themselves subtly invade and destroy the plant.

Herdsmen in the Rocky Mountains are accustomed to seeing large trees that have withstood the strong winds with their massive support structure that they have developed in their roots, only to slowly and quietly succumb, day by day, to something as weak and seemingly irrelevant as a small beetle. Mountain pine beetles destroy wide areas of pine forests on the national forests. As these insects tunnel beneath a tree's bark, their larvae disrupt the movement of food produced by the needles, to the roots. They also release chemicals called pheromones that attract the opposite sex, thereby drawing in more beetles to the same tree. More pheromones are then produced, resulting in a mass attack that overcomes the tree's defenses. Similar attacks are then spread to adjacent trees. Usually within a year of these infestations, the needles will have turned red, indicative of a dead or dying tree.[34]

It is tragic to see the widespread destruction of entire forests of pine trees, which can grow over a hundred feet high. Not only do they present a scene of death and decay, but they also provide an ideal environment for horrific forest fires. Entire herds (or bands) of sheep can be destroyed by a single fire because they refuse to move if the temperature gets too hot. At the base of all of this destruction is a small, otherwise harmless little beetle that the mighty pine tree initially seems to show no recognition as a threat to its very existence.

Animals, like plants, naturally protect themselves from perceived aggressors. Wildlife will go to great extremes to defend themselves against a threat or attack. Herdsmen in the Rocky Mountains are inclined to give a badger the right of way if one is accosted along a trail because, even though they are rather gentle animals if undisturbed, they can be real bullies when confronted. Badgers are probably nature's toughest animal in this part of the world when it comes to a fight. Some call them nature's "street fighters."

Other animals fight or use various types of weapons, talents, or tricks. Skunks spray a highly repulsive smell, rattlesnakes frighten away aggressors, and if necessary, they will strike with a potentially deadly venom. Porcupines turn their backs to an attacker, thrashing their tails back and forth and embedding their sharp, one-way barbed quills that keep moving inward into the bodies of their victims with enormous pain. Bees and wasps inflict a painful sting. Bugs and coyotes bite, rabbits and deer take advantage of their speed, and other animals such as some species of insects, birds, and lizards adapt their appearance to blend in with their environment in order to escape danger without a fight.

Likewise, humans will use any variety of means to protect themselves, their families, and even their fellow citizens against physical threat or attack. They will challenge their aggressor with physical strength, utilize their mental capacities to make weapons, and create police powers and courts of justice to redress their grievances. But what about those silent enemies that are not immediately visible but can also cause serious injury or death?

Whether it be plant life, animal life, or human life, all forms of life may become sick and die from organisms that are too small for the naked eye to see. Like a small beetle in a large pine tree, flesh-eating bacteria find the climate and the nutrients inside of an animal or a person just right. These bad bacteria, called pathogens, are recognized by the body as "foreign invaders." The body's reaction to these invaders is to send out immune system cells to combat them, and if not too late, the body may overtake the bacteria and recover.[35] Otherwise, severe sickness or even death can occur if the body does not prohibit these pathogenic bacteria from multiplying out of control. Aside from bacteria and viruses, larger organisms such as worms or parasites can have similar effects on the body of an animal or a person.

Nature teaches that some of the greatest dangers in life start with little things, like beetles and bugs, or bacteria and viruses. If they are allowed to remain, they will multiply and eventually take control of plants, animals and humans to the point of death.

The same principle can be applied to the health of one's soul. As with physical forms of life, a little sin, rationalized and unchecked, will grow out of control until it will eventually choke and destroy its host. A single alcoholic beverage can easily become two, and then four, and so on until the user becomes an alcoholic. One harmful drug can readily become a drug habit, and then a drug addiction, and ultimately a lethal drug overdose. A simple equivocation, or half lie, if not checked, will multiply into bold-faced lies, followed by felonious acts of deceit and fraud. A single incident involving pornography, if not controlled, will ripen into addictive acts of immorality, like pheromones in a pine tree.

Just as Mother Nature gives living things built-in and acquired defense mechanisms for protection against unwelcome invaders on our physical bodies, our Creator provides important guidance and direction to ward off attacks on our spiritual health. But like the mighty pine trees, individuals and societies sometimes disregard the damage and ultimate destruction that a simple little sin can inflict upon the integrity of our souls if not checked. Those individuals, families, communities, and nations who are wise develop and exercise the discipline to maintain a sound spiritual character and thereby avoid those activities that place one on the slow but decisive path to destruction.

Endnotes:

33 Griffins, (June 15, 2015). "Why do stinging nettles hurt so much?" *Daily Mail Online*, Retrieved from http://www.dailymail.co.uk/sciencetech/article.

34 Gibson, Kenneth E., *Management Guide for Mountain Pine Beetle*, USDA Forest Service (2004).

35 Food and Drug Administration, *Bad Bug Book, Foodborne Pathogenic Microorganisms and Natural Toxins*, Second Edition. Pathogenic Bacteria: 2012. Retrieved from www.fda.gov/downloads/Food/FoodborneIllnessContaminants/UCM297627.pdf.

Lesson 11

God's Living Spring

A cool small spring, alive and well
      its water clean and pure,
runs on the ground where animals dwell
      and gives their thirst a cure.

This little spring, God's show and tell
      some say it can't endure,
ebbs back in the ground, life's mortal bell
      a lifeless sight for sure.

Is this the end, its life's farewell?
      let's not judge premature,
one look at God's creations dispel
      that he's an amateur.

For way up high God's plan unveil
      dark sky's coverture,
as clouds reclaim this small spring that fell
      in earth's dry sepulcher.

All nature born, death will curtail
    a fact man can't obscure,
fatality end and life prevail
    divine investiture.

And so is man, alive and well
    a babe born clean and pure,
who treads on the earth where time will tell
    that death will come for sure.

But come the rain, snow, sleet or hail
    nature's lessons reassure,
God's stamp on his creations foretell
    death's ending can't endure.

On a warm spring day, an aging herdsman stood out on an open ridge and pointed to a pile of bones that constituted the mortal remains of several sheep that had been hit by lightning ten or twelve years earlier. He looked at his employer and said, "Do you see that pile of bones over there?" His employer acknowledged the white, dried-up bones, whereupon the herder replied, "Those skeletons have been there all this time, and they haven't moved an inch!"

As summer approached, that same herdsman, while trailing his sheep to higher elevations, came upon a little spring of water that rose up from the ground and then silently disappeared back into the earth from where it came. He said to himself, "There it goes. That little spring is gone and exists no more." But then there came to his awareness a great lesson that negates such a dire conclusion. This wasn't the end of life for that small spring. Through miraculous means he could not understand, those decomposed molecules of hydrogen and oxygen were recreated in the sky, and that little spring lives on and on. He then thought, *If those decomposed molecules of hydrogen and oxygen can be recreated in the sky, why not as well the molecular structures than comprise my aging body?* He then walked on to the higher elevations with a greater appreciation of life. We are born, we die, and we are lifted up. And thanks to our Creator's marvelous plan, we walk on to higher levels of glory along the path of our eternal course of existence.[36]

This small spring is not a lone recipient of nature's great miracle. Similar springs of water all across the earth unite together to form streams, and from those streams come rivers, which flow into the mighty oceans. Nature does not discriminate from among its creations which ones will live on and which ones will remain forever dead. Continuing life is given freely to all as a divine gift from nature's Creator.

Man is taught by his Creator that a seed that is sown in the ground must decay in order that it may spring forth in its appointed time to a new, more abundant state of existence.[37] The plant that created the seed may have died a violent death, or from a lingering disease or other physical malady, but the plant that comes forth is clean and free of such imperfections.

Nature teaches that newborn animals can also be born into this life without the physical impairments of their ancestors. Human beings who are born with handicaps and other deficiencies are capable of producing offspring that are free of such disorders. Likewise, the deceased and decayed bodies of all humankind will one day rise again with uncorrupted, immortal bodies. There will be no eyes that cannot see, no ears that cannot hear, no need for knee or hip replacements, no heart attacks, no disease, no death.

Such a state of progression is contrary to a law of nature that directs organized matter toward a state of randomness, disorder, and chaos. In the physical world, there is a law of thermodynamics that physicists refer to more specifically as the law of entropy.[38] We see the effects of this law every day. For example, the value and integrity of the houses we reside in and the vehicles we drive do not spontaneously improve over time, but instead trend toward degeneration and unreliability. Gravity causes things to break, and friction causes things to wear out. Without maintenance and occasional repair, such assets will proceed to such a state of disorderliness that they eventually lose all value for the purpose for which they were created.

All forms of organized matter throughout the universe are subject to this law of entropy and necessitate an intelligent force to counter its deleterious tendency toward disorder and chaos. Even the planets of the universe, if left to themselves, will move through space in wild confusion and ultimate disarray without some type of intervention to maintain order and sustenance, let alone progress.

The mortal creation of our physical bodies is likewise subject to degeneration over time, and our best science can only slow the inevitable movement toward death and decay. However, our Creator did give physical bodies limited healing power to preserve life. Broken bones were given the ability to reunite, lacerations of the flesh could seal together again, sophisticated immune systems could launch a defense against viral infections, and escaping blood could undergo a procedure to seal off leaks in the circulatory system. But despite this incredible power for our physical bodies to heal themselves, this ability was not bestowed without limitations. Our bodies were not given the ability to heal themselves against all injury and disease, and through the aging process, all mortal beings are reminded that one day we will leave this frail existence.

Man's ability to intercede and reverse this constant tendency toward disorder is obviously limited. But our Creator has mastered the ability to counter the physical law of entropy. Having created the universe, He knows how to maintain order and control. Having created the earth, He knows how to maintain day and night and the seasons of the year with precision. He knows how to provide and preserve climatic conditions necessary to sustain life. He knows the cure for every virus, every disease, and every handicap. He even knows how to overcome death.

Modern herdsmen in the western United States come from a foreign country. Since they must leave their families behind, a cell phone becomes a very important means of maintaining contact with their loved ones on those occasions when they are within cell range. By simply pressing on the button of this small apparatus, it becomes energized with power, giving it life, kind of like the spirit of a newborn lamb animates it and gives it life. Although the herdsman cannot see it, he knows that it is there. With that power comes instantaneous communication and knowledge, providing a means of sending and receiving messages and pictures of family and friends from all over the world. Miraculously, this little piece of equipment can even think and draw upon its own memory.[39]

Now the materials that make up this small apparatus can become infected with a virus and may even be destroyed. A horse may step on this small apparatus and break it into small pieces, or it may be dropped in a stream or totally destroyed by fire. But the elements that made it possible for that miracle to come into that herdsman's small camp wagon still exists. An exact re-creation can be produced and placed right back in that herdsman's hands.

In similar fashion the herdsman may ask, if man can re-create this small phone and energize it with power, cannot my Creator re-create me if my physical body dies or is destroyed? Does He not have continuing access to that same supply of elements that He used to create me in the first place? Does He not also have the means or the ability to take that same genetic code now embodied in my living cells with which to format new ones? And with those elements and that genetic code, is He not able to animate that lifeless body with that same spirit that gives my body life today? If my Creator was able to create me in the first place, does He not lack the knowledge and the power to do it again?

The answer to these questions is of course He does. If man can perform such a great miracle with a cell phone, God, our Creator, can certainly re-create us a second time. Who would dare limit God's ability to re-create that which He has created before? He was capable of creating us the first time, and He is equally capable of doing it again.

Endnotes:

36 A similar thought is taken from Smith, Henry A., *Matthew Cowley Man of Faith*, Salt Lake City, Utah: Bookcraft, 1986, 271.

37 See 1 Corinthians 15:36–38.

38 For an explanation of the law of entropy, see Knight, Randall D., *Physics for Scientists and Engineers*, Third Edition, Vol. 1, San Luis Obispo: California Polytechnic State University, 2013, 518–20.

39 See Smith, Henry A., Matthew Cowley Man of Faith, Salt Lake City, Utah: Bookcraft, 1986, 267.

Lesson 12

Nature's Greatest Gift

This world can really be mean.
It can present a horrible scene,
like a leper while only a teen
crying out, "Unclean, unclean."

Our plants may carry a blight,
or our animals could get a mite,
and as humans our mortal plight
is struggling with all our might.

But nature was given a plan
to lift up earth and mortal man
so that all God's creations can
live life better than they began.

God sent a Savior to redeem
His creations from everything
that a temporal life does bring
by His almighty hand supreme.

This is a world in which all living things inherit the seeds of death. A shepherd witnesses all forms of disease, malformation, and death among various forms of plant and animal life every day. Among the animals over which he is given direct responsibility, he is constantly challenged with how best to deal with corruptible flesh, and too often he finds that his challenge is beyond repair. Recognizing that all things will eventually die, the assurance of life after death in a refined and perfected state of existence must, the shepherd concludes, be the greatest of all gifts that could be bestowed on living things.

As referenced earlier, there is comfort in the thought that a person's body may rise from the grave just as any decaying seed may spring forth out of the ground and give that same plant new life.[40] Even those plants that have been afflicted with disease or physical deformity are given the gift of a new life that is entirely free of such defects, recognizing, of course, that a noxious weed will always spring back into life as the same variety of noxious weed, and that a beautiful flower will find renewed life with all its beauty and magnificence fully restored.

As a shepherd witnesses the death of diseased and deformed plant life all around him, he also sees those same plants spring back from the ground into a new and vigorous life that is fully free of infirmity, and he receives assurance that he too may one day spring back into life with a physical body that is free of exhaustion and fatigue.

"Assuming that I too may rise from the ground into a new and vigorous life that is free of deformity, disease, and exhaustion, what can I expect my living conditions to be like," the shepherd contemplates. "I have not lived a perfect life, and I am plagued with this so-called 'worm that shall not die.'[41] Will my spirit that will one day be housed within a perfected physical body also be reborn free and clear of all impurity? As is apparently the case of the imperfections of my physical body, is there also a process by which the spirit that houses my physical body can be freed of imperfections so that I can mingle with others who have unblemished characters?"

His Creator replies, "When you were a child and rebelled against your parents, you wanted to know that they still loved you, and they did. Likewise, my heart continues to hold tender feelings toward you, and I have designed a plan by which you may not only be freed of your physical defects and frailties but of your spiritual imperfections as well, just as your mortal parents devised plans to help you overcome your shortcomings."

The shepherd looks at his surroundings and recognizes that nature utilizes two great cleansing agents to remove the filthiness of corruption, fire and water.[42] When forests and other forms of plant life are infected with a disease, nature sends lightning to rid herself of such impurity. But the process is not easy. While fire cleanses the disease, its smoke in turn pollutes the air, which in turn must then become purified. Therefore, our Creator ordained a hydrological cycle that takes water molecules from the oceans and great lakes and streams and places them into the atmosphere, and then back to the land and the ocean. During this process, as raindrops fall toward the ground, they attract numerous particles, thereby acting to purify and clean the air of pollutants. In the end, all the disease and impurity is removed.

"But," the shepherd insists, "can water and fire cleanse my soul of all impurity?" He then realizes that while fire can destroy his physical body and all the disease and physical impurity that resides within it, a cleansing of his body by fire will only cause his spirit to depart and will do nothing to destroy it or free it of impurity. Similarly, water can cleanse the physical body of filth and various forms of dirty matter, but it takes something more to cleanse the spirit. While these two natural cleansing agents are used symbolically to cleanse the spirit, there yet remains the fact that they are mere symbols. "What then will it take to rid my soul of all these imperfections?" the shepherd asks. *Surely,* he thinks, *nature's physical cleansing agents will not suffice as spiritual cleansing agents as well.*

His Creator subtly assures him that his observations are correct, drawing his attention to His account of the days of Noah when the earth was cleansed and all but eight souls were destroyed by water,[43] and also to His warning that fire will one day be used in a day yet to come to once again cleanse the earth of impurity.[44] But these accounts, the shepherd concludes, cleanse the earth but say nothing about purging the filth and wickedness from the souls of those wicked persons who are destroyed by water or fire.

"Perhaps," the shepherd reasons, "there is some formula that the lessons of nature do not visibly teach that can purify sin." He contemplates that our Creator's record speaks of miracles that are not visibly apparent from the eternal laws of nature, such as an account of a man named Joshua who bid the sun to stand still and it was done,[45] or of Moses who parted the Red Sea,[46] or of Enoch who moved mountains and caused rivers to change their course.[47] Even greater, he recalls, is an account of Elijah who raised a widow's son from the dead,[48] and of Peter who restored the woman Tabitha back to life, though still destined to mortality.[49] "But," he then concludes, "why is there no account of any great man who purged away the sins of a wicked person?" His Creator gently reminds him that certain lessons of nature can only be understood from the higher, spiritual level of understanding and are generally considered foolishness to the person who seeks learning from the lesser, physical sphere.[50] These are lessons that are only taught in the upper-division courses of those who qualify as students of the spiritual realm.

And then the shepherd understands that such an accomplishment is beyond the capability of men or angels and that "only one name under heaven" has the ability to fulfill such a task.[51] Therefore, our

Creator personally entered this physical sphere of His own creation and somehow overcame mortality, raising not only His body from the dead but the bringing of all of His mortal creations with Him.[52] While others could act as God's agent in performing mighty miracles, even in restoring a lifeless body back to mortal life, only He could extend to all nature the greatest of all the gifts of God, the gift of immortality and eternal life.

But this does not mean that all those who suffer spiritual death will be restored with a spiritually spotless bill of health as is the case with physical death. No person, the shepherd recognizes, is required to conform his character to fit in with that society where our Creator dwells. Surely there are many who do not desire to adhere to the standards of a society peopled by those who obey the laws of righteousness. It is inconsistent to suggest that upon death the depravity of a tyrant who preys upon the innocent will be suddenly washed clean of his propensity for evil. Surely a person with evil designs would, if allowed entrance, infuse wickedness into a society comprised of otherwise righteous individuals.

The shepherd ponders the fact that a container of pure water will not remain pure if polluted gray water is poured into its contents. As water cannot remain pure if exposed to contamination, the shepherd concludes, no righteous society can sustain itself if populated by unrighteous people.

But what if the owner of that same container of gray water were to create a filtering device to make his water clean, just as nature's streams flush out her impurities with the rough flow of contaminated waters over her rocky soils? Even if such water must percolate within the depths of the ground for a time, can it not arise from that dark aquifer, clean and pure? And is it not true that this refined water can then be comingled with the water of a pure container without the risk of contamination? Does nature not teach that dirty water that has passed through her redeeming process can become clean and pure, just as if no such contamination had occurred in the first place?

Relating this analogy to life after death, it requires one who is vested with seeds of immortality to filter the seed of death out of a mortal being. It also requires one who is clean and free of all imperfection to filter the vile and the dross out of an imperfect soul. Because no mortal human being fits such unique qualifications, this is a mission that only our Creator could fulfill. Such a marvelous gift could never be bestowed by one who could not bridge the gap between mortality and immortality, and between perfection and imperfection.

This greatest of all gifts, the shepherd acknowledges, cannot be proved by physical observance or experimentation. Our Creator's record says, for example, that two major events of earth's natural history took place in two separate gardens. The first of these was a garden that our Creator is said to have planted all forms of life, a garden known as the garden of Eden.[53] This was a place of pristine innocence and beauty, a place that knew neither death nor decay, but that provided neither for procreation nor for a knowledge of the difference between good and evil. Modern scientists take no notice that such a garden ever existed because, they say, there is no proof. Of course, they are likewise incapable of proving that such a garden did not exist.

According to our Creator's record, the earth subsequently fell into a lower sphere of existence that brought with it all the mortal elements of disease, aging, death, and decay that we experience in our world today. With these truths, all humankind is intimately familiar.

The second great event is said to have taken place in another garden called Gethsemane.[54] It was there that our Creator planted the seeds of immortality and eternal life. Following His own natural law, only He could plant those seeds because only He had inherited those eternal traits of immortality from His father. His mortal mother gave Him the ability to suffer a physical death, which our Creator likewise inherited from her. Vested with both the ability to die and the ability to live on into immortality, our Creator somehow miraculously provided a pathway for all humankind to obtain a resurrected body through His mercy and grace. Further, putting off the "natural man" with all its accompanying carnal instincts and following His word, all humankind is permitted to avail themselves of His purifying process that He devised for us to be free of all our uncleanliness, thereby entitling us to an eternal association in the society of the righteous.

This greatest of all gifts is freely available to all living things. It is available to men, women, and children of every generation, race, and ethnicity. It is freely offered to the strong and the weak, the rich and the poor, the bond and the free, the sinner and the saint.

According to our Creator's record, we learn in the forty-sixth chapter of Genesis that because of their occupations as shepherds, the sons of Jacob were not allowed to dwell near the Egyptians in Egypt, for they were regarded as unclean. The stigma of this occupation has not changed over time. At the time of our Creator's birth, shepherds were considered to be on the lowest rung of the social ladder. These lowly men were not only considered to be unclean physically; they were also deemed as unclean spiritually since their work precluded them from association with those who regularly attended the temple and the synagogues. Even to this day, herdsmen are given this social mark of disgrace, being physically unclean because they are untidy and dirty and spiritually unclean because they live and work far from any man-made house of worship.

The shepherd's mind refers back to earlier lessons. He again recognizes that despite their reputations among men, our Creator appeared to the shepherd Moses in the burning bush, He chose the young shepherd David as the king of Israel, and He had His angels appear to shepherds in the field to add glory and celebration to His own birth in the meridian of time. Perhaps this reminder serves as an invitation from our Creator to all, "let him that is athirst come. And whosoever will, let him take the water of life freely."[55]

This "water of life" is not of a physical nature. All things, both temporal and spiritual, were created and made to bear record of our Creator. Some of these records are not written in the natural man's language but are apprehended only on a higher sphere or level of understanding. They are lessons that are taught within the silence of the student's heart and inner mind, unobstructed by the noise and confusion of conflicting ideas or doctrines.

Endnotes:

40 Ibid.

41 Mark 9:48

42 See Robinson, James M., "Gospel of Phillip," Nag Hammadi Library, San Fransisco, California: Harper & Row Publishers, 1981, 135.

43 1 Peter 3:20

44 Malachi 4:1

45 Joshua 10:12

46 Exodus 14:21

47 Moses 6:8

48 1 Kings 17:23

49 Acts 9:40

50 1 Corinthians 2:14

51 Acts 4:11–12

52 1 Corinthians 15:20–22; Acts 24:15

53 Genesis 2:8

54 Matthew 26:36; John 18:1

55 Revelation 22:17

Lesson 13

God's Natural Law

A natural law is a heavenly right
    that men may sometimes deny.
As basic as light, when taken men fight,
    a right for which they will die.

God's charge from above is what we think of
    with this law that we travel by.
It's the sign of the dove, symbolic of love
    as clear as the clear blue sky.

This code in our hearts makes evil depart
    and runs tyranny awry.
Implicitly part of what makes humans start
    to honor men eye to eye.

Take access to air, or infantile care
    or water when we're dry.
As humans we eat, we drink and we sleep,
    these rights we should never deny.

The propagation of race, its time and place
      are tenets we justify.
No life can be erased except in the case
      one murders another guy.

These natural rights are what some men despite
      for no legitimate cause.
With courage and might such tyrants take flight,
      along with their selfish flaws.

When English kings caused their subjects to bring
      a paper that they did write,
A marvelous thing from which justice did spring
      it was called their Bill of Rights.

Those kings clearly owed this bill's moral code
      to those men that had to die,
but no force could implode that sacred road
      we hail as fourth of July.

Is this now the day when freedom, we pray
      won't echo that battle cry?
Our liberty bell is not up for sale,
      these rights came from God on High.

An elderly man told of an experience he had as a boy who grew up on a sheep ranch. He said that when he was young, he enjoyed racing horses through a meadow with his brother. On one such occasion, the boys' horses sped out of control along a trail in the direction of a patch of trees. As his horse approached a giant aspen tree, he mustered all of his strength and gave the big white trunk of the tree a push to protect his leg from injury as his horse sped by. Only years later did he take notice that it was not the massive tree that was displaced, but the horse on which he was riding.

As the universal laws of nature cannot be removed or displaced, there is another set of laws that, like the giant aspen tree, remain unmoved. But unlike the universal laws of nature, our Creator allows us to reject or push aside these laws as we travel through life. He gives humankind the agency to choose between abiding by their strictures and mandates or proceeding against them, the violation of which will lead to physical or emotional distress. This group of laws is commonly referred to as natural law. Philosophers commonly describe natural law as a system of right or justice held to be common to all humans and derived from nature rather than from the rules of society,[56] the latter of which is commonly referred to as "positive law."[57]

As applied to a shepherd who lives alone with his animals, natural law deals with how he cares for them. These laws may or may not be independent of the terms of his employment, but they are commonly accepted within the community as inherent rules of humanity or in the case of shepherds, animal husbandry. By way of example, a herdsman need not be taught that animals within his care are entitled to eat when hungry, to drink when thirsty, or to rest when they get tired. Even a hard-hearted individual knows that it is wrong to inexcusably beat an animal to the point of serious injury or death, the consequence of which is a violation of that animal's inherent rights.

Although natural law is typically related to human relationships, it also applies to animals. Some animals are vicious, predatory creatures by nature, but they too subscribe to natural law. Take, for example, a pack of wolves. They have a very strict level of hierarchy that has to be honored by all members of the pack; otherwise, unity and social order would fail. The alpha male is the leader, and its mate is the beta female. Each member in a pack has a job to do, and by each fulfilling its respective role, they develop strong physical and emotional bonds. At the center of their collective attention is the need to eat. Wolves are carnivores (meat eaters), and so they kill. As such, they are very dangerous to other forms of wildlife and domesticated animals, such as sheep. But despite their innate nature to kill, they long for interaction with each other and rarely hurt or fight other wolves within their pack. Only when food is scarce are they inclined to exert physical force on other wolves outside of their pack.[58]

Natural law supports a use of force to protect one's natural rights. If a deer nibbling on some forbs suddenly catches a glimpse of a cougar hiding in a thicket of trees, it will not attack the cougar but will impulsively flee the area for the protection of its life. The cougar, on the other hand, will justify its need to kill the deer for the reason that its biological nature requires that it eat meat to stay alive. So one may ask, is not the deer's natural right to life violated by the cougar acting on its innate nature to kill it in order to satisfy its hunger? And is it a violation of the cougar's right to life for a herdsman to kill a cougar to protect the lives of his sheep? Despite best intentions, the infliction of death on both plants and animals is the nature of the temporal world in which we live.

Likewise, a human being does not violate an animal's natural rights if he kills for food or protects some other legitimate human right, such as self-defense. As space, time, and matter are predicated upon universal laws of nature, so is the distinct nature of a human being predicated on those natural laws with which his Creator endowed him since birth. A human being is formed by his Creator as an omnivore, a person who eats both animal and vegetable substances. Therefore, he is justified by natural law to kill an animal for the purpose of satisfying his hunger.

Similar yet distinct from the animal kingdom, man is a rational, a social, and a property-owning individual. Natural law recognizes this mix of man's distinct qualities. Consequently, human beings are endowed by their Creator with the right to life, liberty, and property, and with the commensurate right to protect themselves against those who would kill or enslave them, or steal their property.

Human beings recognize force or violence as a reality of life, and they are instinctively endowed with the cognitive means of recognizing when their basic rights may be violated. A herdsman may immediately sense the threat of the sound of a rattle and impulsively throw a stick or a large rock in the direction of a rattlesnake that is coiled and ready to strike. Likewise, a person on a city street may sense danger upon seeing a suspiciously dressed man with a pistol or a knife and may therefore use whatever force or physical means he has to defend himself. Or an entire country may sense a threat from an enemy and justify protection of its society's natural rights with the use of military force.

But of course, natural law does not allow one to indiscriminately force or kill another, whether it be an animal or another human. We are given a faculty by which we can pass judgment on our own conduct, either approving or condemning it, and to thereby anticipate the divine judgment from our Creator based on our actions. This faculty, or conscience, is inborn with every human being and is a natural capacity to distinguish between good and evil.[59]

An integral tenet of Christianity is the principle that natural rights are vested by "divine province" and are outside the authority or license of other men to violate.[60] While our Creator has given humankind the ability to violate or ignore the natural rights of others, decisions that are centered on basic physical desire confine humankind to the lowest or physical sphere of existence. This is the penalty for noncompliance. As natural rights are honored, humankind is elevated to the higher, moral realm. Natural law dictates how people should behave among each other. These laws form essential elements in humanity's well-being. Laws based on such concepts as justice rather than injustice, and mercy rather than harshness, form the soul and substance of life.

As applied to communities and nations, these laws are based on the theory or belief that certain rights exist independently of any societal granting of those rights. Natural law vests rights in individuals that cannot be revoked, amended, or withdrawn by majority vote. If animals could vote, no shepherd would recognize any justice in allowing two coyotes and a sheep to vote on what to have for dinner, although the killing of a sheep to eat would not be contrary to the coyotes' innate behavior. Likewise, no group of people, regardless of size or similarity, would be justified in submitting the natural rights of an individual within its society to popular vote unless for a legitimate cause, such as punishment for a perpetrator's crime.

Violations of natural law are typically called into issue whenever a group rebels against their government and asserts rights to which they are entitled by their Creator but which their society or government refuses to grant them. A ruler who violates natural law is illegitimate for the reason that he has no right to be obeyed. Rulers who act in violation of natural law are nature's criminals and should be dealt with in accordance with natural law. In other words, nature teaches that such rulers are like dangerous animals, the common enemies of humankind, and are worthy of punishment.

People who believe they are endowed by their Creator with certain rights base their claims on natural or God-given law, while those who reject such inalienable rights base their beliefs on positive or man-made law.[61] Positive law stands for the proposition that man has no rights unless granted to him from the government, and no action is inherently right or wrong under the law unless there is legislative or court-created law that says so. By way of example, those who reject natural law would claim that murder isn't illegal because it is "evil" or bad, but that murder is illegal because there is a written law in the books that says so.

A government that is structured on positive law has no moorings beyond the present attitude of those people who create and uphold it. As opposed to political leaders who concentrate on fulfilling their ministerial duties based on moral principles and adherence to natural law, those who reject natural law lean toward ruling by force. It can be a dangerous government, symbolically likened to a pack of wolves preying on the innocent sheep. Like a thin crust over a bubbling volcano, a government that justifies its actions on positive law may erupt without prediction at any time. History contains many instances of entire societies that are subjected to the unstable demands of positive law, such as history's descriptions of the self-serving king, or a tyrannical dictator who grants or denies rights at his pleasure.

The history of England serves as an example of the consequences of positive law. The harsh rule of William II and Henry I culminated in the year 1100 with a document called the Charter of Liberties, the first clear forerunner of the US Constitution. Continuing denial of natural rights throughout that century resulted in a civil war and a demand on King John to sign the Magna Carta (a Latin term for "Great Charter") in 1215, which document constitutes the underpinnings of what we recognize today as the rule of law.[62] The rule of law is a legal concept that recognizes that men are most free when governed by law rather than by men, the main idea being that when both the rulers and the ruled are subjected to the same law, despotic power can be curtailed.

As the history of England evolved, failure to honor the mandates of the Magna Carta led to further protest.[63] Kings like Henry VIII wielded unrestrained power and Queen Mary I had almost three hundred people burned at the stake for taking exception to her religious views, earning her the name "Bloody Mary." By 1628, political oppression had progressed to the point where parliament convened to deliver to the king a document called the Petition of Right, which served as a model for America's Declaration of Independence a century and a half later. Charles I would not accept the Petition of Right, so he dissolved parliament and led the country into further revolt at a time that the Pilgrims were leaving England to settle in America. By 1685, the struggle for power reached a crisis stage under King James II. In 1689, when William and Mary aspired to the throne, they were obliged to agree to a list of conditions that were set forth in a document called the Declaration of Rights, later reenacted as the Bill of Rights.[64]

In the United States, the political application of natural law is spelled out in clear terms in its Bill of Rights, first created in England during the reign of William and Mary and acknowledged in principle by the founding fathers of the US government in the preamble of the Declaration of Independence, a declaration to the world that asserts the basic right to be free. The US Constitution, remarkable as it was, initially failed to include a specific declaration—or bill—of individual rights. It spelled out what the respective branches of government could do but did not specify what it could not do, such as placing certain restrictions on speech, or on the press, or the right to peaceably assemble or to worship God according to the dictates of one's conscience. Consequently, the Bill of Rights adopted in the United States is remarkably similar to its English predecessor created from hard lessons learned across the Atlantic.[65]

These historic documents that set forth those inalienable rights that our Creator has decreed as basic to human life define the limitations of moral government. The question is whether governmental leaders will honor these keystone documents that are designed to protect the natural rights of its citizens. Will the moral principles of government that are set forth in the US Constitution be discarded as archaic or inconsistent with modern trends? Even the lowliest class of individuals, the humble herdsmen, can see warning signs that predict a denial of basic human liberties as moral principles give way to positive law.

Endnotes:

56 Editors of *Encyclopedia Britannica*. (Feb. 16, 2010). Natural Law, Encyclopedia Britannica. Retrieved from https://www.britannica.com/topic/natural-law.

57 *Black's Law Dictionary*, "Positive Law." 1046 (rev. 5th ed. 1979).

58 Report issued by U.S. Fish & Wildlife Service, Grey Wolf Biologue, USFWS Ecological Service's Field Offices in the Upper Midwest, last updated Sept. 12. 2016.

59 See John 1:4, 8–9; 8:12

60 Application of natural law may be regarded as a Christian's version of the Golden Rule as Christ directed His followers in Matthew 7:12.

61 Inalienable or unalienable refers to that which cannot be given away or taken away. The unalienable rights that are mentioned in the Declaration of Independence could just as well have been inalienable, which means the same thing.

62 For a discussion in the role of the Magna Carta in the rule of law as recognized in the United States, see Perry, Richard L., under general supervision of Cooper, John C., *Sources of Our Liberties*, Chicago, Illinois: American Bar Association, 1978, 11–22.

63 Lieberman, Jethro K., *The Enduring Constitution*, West Publishing Company: Saint Paul, Minn., 1987, 9–12.

64 In his concurring judgment in the case of Department of Transportation v. Association of American Railroads, 135 S.Ct. 1225, ___ U.S.___, 191 L.Ed.2d 153 (2015), Justice Thomas opined that the concept of the rule of law has been understood as far back as Greek and Roman times to mean that a ruler must be subject to the law in exercising his power and may not govern by will alone.

65 Menard, Albert, *Fundamentals of Public Law*, Moscow, Idaho: College of Law, University of Idaho, 1980, 93-94.

Lesson 14

Perfection in Embryo

Part I: The Government of God

The government of God, alive and well;
    its order, beauty and grandeur excel.
Stars send their message and each day they tell,
    of a master plan no man can dispel.

    It's no secret in the expanse of space,
        that planets revolve with speed and with grace.
    Perfect in timing they move in their place,
        brilliantly patterned to maintain their pace.

    Here on our earth is the day and the night,
        summer and winter, and air temp just right.
    Punctually lighted to give us our sight,
        coated with moisture at just the right height.

    Plants in all their varieties we find,
        they propagate strictly after their kind.
    They live and then die, and perfectly timed,
        spring forth again not one season behind.

The beasts of the field and fouls of the air,
    the fish in the sea, the bugs and the bear--
no artist can paint or rightly compare
    God's infinite greatness is everywhere.

But where then stands man, God's greatest on earth,
    formed in His image and priceless in worth?
Fallen from grace amidst evil from birth,
    but destined to rise in His universe.

Like fire refines, perfection takes time
    to rise above greed, corruption and crime.
Casting off evil, we'll grow to our prime
    clothing the naked and leading the blind.

Out of the smog and glare of city lights, shepherds have clear view of the night skies and cannot help but notice the regularity of the stars' existence and the timeliness and precision of the earth's movement. Thanks to our scientists, we know that our earth, as one of nine planets that revolves around our sun, travels through space at a tremendous speed of about 67,000 miles per hour. Scientists have determined that the earth's 584 million–mile trip around the sun requires 365 days, 6 hours, 9 minutes, and 10 seconds to complete its sidereal or astronomical year. In all the years that we have knowledge of, never has our earth been as much as one second late in completing its scheduled revolution around the sun.[66]

No less remarkable is the precise timing by which our days and nights and the seasons of our year are governed. A day and night are completed every time the earth makes one revolution on its axis, taking 23 hours, 56 minutes, and 4 seconds while at the same time consistently spinning at a linear speed 1,036 miles per hour as measured from its equator.[67] Added to this precision in its rotation at such a terrific speed, the earth methodically adjusts its tilt toward the sun over the course of a year. This axial tilt changes the inclination of the sun's trajectory, thereby giving us our seasons. Consequently, when the North Pole is tilted toward the sun, a person in the northern latitude would notice the sun higher in the sky and experience longer days. Since more solar radiation would reach the earth's surface, average temperatures would also be warmer. Conversely, when the North Pole is tilted away from the sun, the reverse is true and the days would be shorter and generally cooler.[68] This is why the Arctic Circle experiences no daylight at all for a part of the year, which is called a polar night.

The shepherd looks at the surface of the earth where his sheep are grazing and cannot help but feel a deep appreciation for the manner in which the surface of the earth is organized. The make and construction of the various forms of plant and animal life are each adapted to their particular environments, all controlled by their Creator's wisdom and power, fully independent of man. The conformation of the grasses and shrubs, the flowers and trees, the birds and the beasts, the fishes and the reptiles, are all striking exemplifications of the existence of a Creator with knowledge and wisdom that far exceeds our own.

After the waters were separated from the land, the biblical record indicates that the earth was prepared to support plant and animal life.[69] On the land, topsoil was provided as a natural seedbed for plant life.[70] As earth's first horticulturalist, our Creator planted a garden eastward in Eden that produced all varieties of plant life.[71] Likewise, as the earth's first practitioner of animal husbandry, He placed all manner of animal life in His garden.[72] All of these creations, according to the biblical record, were created in an incorruptible state, not subject to death, aging, pain, sorrow, or corruption of any kind.[73]

But then, our Creator's record says the earth and all of those creations on, above, and below the land fell from its faultless state of existence into a lower gradient of life.[74] All of God's creations were now subjected to misery, pain, sorrow, and death, all according to His will. But why would a perfect God allow such a thing to happen? If man can see evidence of God's perfect system of government all around him, why should such a state of corruption be allowed to exist in His environment? A shepherd sees a severely wounded sheep that has been viciously attacked by a violent predator and asks, why would a loving Creator allow such an innocent victim of terror to suffer such an attack?

Is there no value in understanding the difference between good and bad, in experiencing pain and suffering in order that joy and happiness can be appreciated? Can one fully appreciate justice without witnessing injustice? Is there not provided an opportunity for growth as man learns how to overcome evil? Can a society not benefit from learning how to evolve from the immoral effects of brute force and tyranny into a government that is based on moral principles of justice?

Despite the state of corruption based on survival of the fittest that exists among God's creations on earth, there still remains in plain view those qualities of comfort and perfection that provide not only guidance, but security and continuity along the pathway to a better life. Essential elements to sustain life from generation to generation are preserved. Despite the noxious weeds that now grow on earth, beautiful and productive plants remain and spring back into life year after year. Despite the pests and other forms of animal life that harass and distress man, all varieties of desirous animals reproduce after their own kind, thereby providing each generation of man with the opportunity to enjoy the benefits of their existence. To ensure continuing plant and animal life, our Creator has ordained that an adequate layer of topsoil be maintained.

Earth's ability to retain its topsoil depth is illustrious of the magnificence of God's creations. Modern-day herdsmen in the Rocky

Mountains of the western United States typically trail their sheep down from the high elevations as winter approaches, where they are pastured on fields that are seeded to such crops as alfalfa and small grains. These fields are rarely fallowed and produce crops under a rotation that often includes potatoes, for which Idaho is well-known. Herdsmen eat potatoes as a part of their staple diet and have a basic knowledge of how potatoes are grown. A herdsman may ask, how can this earth, upon which his sheep come home to graze year after year, continue to produce good crops without depleting the topsoil?

A crop of potatoes with a three-year rotation on a 120-acre parcel will produce roughly eighty-three million pounds over a fifty-year period. The Russet Burbank that is grown in Idaho has a high solid, low moisture content. This is often referred to as specific gravity, which typically ranges from 8 to 9 percent and that, if converted into pounds over a fifty-year period on a three-year rotation, equates to approximately seven hundred thousand pounds (thirty-five thousand tons) of solid matter. One may reasonably ask, should the depth of this farmer's soil not diminish over time? Amazingly, without taking into account the thousands of tons of other crops produced during that fifty-year period, not one inch of his soil depth is lost.

Next consider that an Idaho potato is comprised of about 92 percent water.[75] No crop, including potatoes, can mature without water at regular intervals during the growth period. Potatoes require about one to two inches of water per week. An acre foot of water weighs 225,060 pounds. If Mother Nature is reluctant to supply the necessary water, then some type of supplemental water source is required. To accommodate this need, our Creator has supplemented man's needs with a vast quantity of water from an underground aquifer from which water can be drawn to provide the right amount of moisture at precisely the right time.

Leaving potatoes aside, our world has been created in such a manner as to provide an endless variety of beauty and magnificence. We have oceans and deserts, lakes and forests, small streams and large rivers, mountains and grasslands, all of which are arranged and sustained for the comfort and enjoyment of humans.

The planets that move majestically in a perfect system of order and harmony within their respective spheres are the result of our Creator's divine intelligence and wisdom.[76] He governs, not only the heavens above, but the earth beneath. He created the plants and the trees in all their varieties. He created the fish, the fowls, the insects, the beasts, and all other forms of animal life that cover the earth. Last, He created man, both male and female, in His own image and likeness. All of these creations are subject to His laws and controlled at His direction. None of these creations were organized by chance, but all of this was done in the councils of God, as testified by the apostle Paul to the Colossians:

> For by him were all things created, that are in heaven, and that are in earth, visible and invisible, whether they be thrones, or dominions, or principalities, or powers: all things were created by him, and for him: And he is before all things, and by him all things consist.[77]

Surely that young shepherd of old who undoubtedly acquired the habit of deep reflection while surrounded in the silence of tending to his sheep, appropriately expressed his gratitude to God, when he, as King David later proclaimed:

> When I consider thy heavens, the work of thy fingers, the moon and the stars, which thou hast ordained; What is man, that thou art mindful of him? ... For

thou hast made him a little lower than the angels, and has crowned him with glory and honor. Thou madest him to have dominion over the works of thy hands; though hast put all things under his feet.[78]

With this dominion our Creator allows mortal man to freely use, it is important that we use His creations wisely. By focusing our activities on a course that is reconcilable with our Creator's will, we can avoid the corruption that constitutes the penalty for noncompliance with the laws by which our universe is governed.

Part II: The Government of Man

The government of man, alive and well;
    sprinkled from heaven but mired in hell.
As despots who reign will ruthlessly yell,
    step to the line at the sound of my bell!

Each to his own, and the best man to win
    love verses hate among closest of kin.
Virtue cleaves virtue while sin begets sin,
    regret and sorrow o're what might have been.

Countries beat countries and clamor for gain,
    the trodden seek food and shelter in vain.
The rich have their plenty but labor in pain,
    and nothing has changed since the days of Cain.

Is man but an earthly being alone,
    destined to die in oblivion unknown?
Bruised in the body and worked to the bone,
    to live and die with no soul of his own?

No! We are spirits begotten of God,
    clothed with a body that came from the sod.
With glimpses of glory far from abroad,
    we'll cling to the truth like an iron rod.

It isn't our lot to vanish from space,
    and live out our lives in utter disgrace.
Each challenge and burden we'll proudly face,
    until we arrive in that perfect place.

Until then we plunder, we steal and kill.
    But one day when man submits to God's will,
and earth takes glory, its measure fulfill
    order and harmony, and peace be still.

What could a lowly, socially awkward shepherd know about modern-day government? Modern societies elect smart and influential leaders with advanced degrees from the most prestigious universities to enact, enforce, and adjudicate laws, people who are trained in political procedure, domestic and foreign affairs, military strategy and social behavior. What could an unsophisticated, uneducated shepherd contribute to such a complex arrangement of human affairs? One answer may lie in a simple shepherd's ability to contrast his appreciation for our Creator's perfect system of government with that of the man-made governments of the world.

As a shepherd quietly contemplates his surroundings, it occurs to him that nature has vested the planet earth with three great kingdoms of nature: the mineral kingdom, the plant kingdom, and the animal kingdom. Leaving a large boulder on which he was patiently sitting next to a creek, he proceeds down a trail along the fast-flowing water.

Suddenly he notices a beautiful, rounded pebble in the stream, and his attention is immediately drawn to the first of these three great kingdoms. His thoughts go back to the words of an ancient prophet named Job, who once said, "stones shall speak," and he proceeds to ask the small, round pebble how it got to be so smooth and polished. Of course, he knows that this pebble does not speak his language any more than the dog at his side or the birds in the pine trees. He must learn that the rocks and stones speak of their past history with their looks rather than by their sound, and that his mind must act as the interpreter between their language and his.

The pebble then proceeds to tell its story. "I am similar in appearance to the big boulder you sat on upstream," it said, "and I was torn loose by the stream and came rolling down to where you found me."

The shepherd then realizes that the farther he walks down the stream, the smaller the pebbles in the water appear to be with the declining speed of the water. The pebble then says, "The other pebbles that I was with in the water came from other locations, such as from overhanging cliffs or from below the earth's surface as the stream has gradually cut its way down the canyon." And finally, the pebble says, "As the fast-flowing water has moved us along over the years, we have been jostled, tumbled, and rolled over and over down the stream, and this is what made me smooth and round."

The shepherd then responds, "You're just like humans, because we too tend to get our rough edges made smooth by the design of our Creator to mingle and struggle in our relationships with other people, especially after we've been tumbled and bounced around for a quite some time."

Like that small pebble, he recognizes that many people have assembled together in this country from various locations and circumstances, including himself. "I must be one of the smallest of pebbles, given that I have settled for a time in this foreign country, far from home, and only a little and insignificant guy at the bottom of the social scale," he determines. "But this is all right because in my youth, I came here broken away from my home, ragged and untidy, but day by day my ignorance is being chipped away in this rough and tumble world. The beautiful truth of my existence is becoming exposed, and in the process, my surface is becoming polished and smooth. And though I am small in stature and strength," he concludes, "I am becoming among the most beautiful of God's creations."

As the shepherd leaves the upper elevations of the creek, he passes through a large grove of lodgepole pine trees that had been growing together since before his birth. His thoughts leave the mineral kingdom and turn to the plant kingdom. "These trees have grown straight and tall," he notices, "far different from the massive tree I see growing all alone behind me up on that hill." He then realizes, "Clearly, these trees that have grown together will make the best lumber, quite unlike that lone tree up on the hill that has so many branches that, if it were cut into boards, would be full of knots and poor in quality." Suddenly he realized that his character, if not carefully nurtured, could ultimately turn out just like that rough and gnarled tree.

"But are trees that grow in close-knit groves always a good thing?" the shepherd asks. "Perhaps there is a reason that the gigantic old tree that is off on its own still survives. What if one of the large old trees in this grove gets infected with a bug or a virus? Does this not bring the entire community of trees in peril of a similar attack? Or what if a blight enters the grove with a fungal infection? Or if a lightning strikes the tallest tree in this grove, is it not true that all the other trees within its community are more likely to burn than that rugged old tree that is off on its own? Societies of people, like groves of trees, can either live and grow together or suffer and die together," the shepherd concludes.

This simple-minded shepherd then observes his sheep and focuses his attention on nature's animal kingdom. He asks himself, "Why do animals fight?" This question may not be difficult to answer if it is recognized that animals typically base their thinking on impressions obtained through their physical senses without regard to moral consequences. Even sheep, which are regarded as rather mild and nonaggressive, tend to conduct their actions within the physical realm of learning. Each year the time comes for the male sheep to prove to all the other males who is boss. This calls for a lot of fighting. Mother Nature has provided Rocky Mountain bighorn sheep and domesticated Rambouillet rams with curled horns for use as weapons as they seek to acquire dominance or mating rights.[79] The clash of their horns can be heard from a distance as these powerful animals rear back on their legs and then simultaneously run toward each other at full speed.

It is common for other animals to fight as well. Take the well-known robin, for example, the great North American songbird. Most people regard robins as having gentle, yet lively dispositions. But a study of these birds will not always present a gentle picture. When robins claim a patch of land as their own, likely for its good source of food and shelter, they will not tolerate another robin entering their area unless, of course, the other bird happens to be a mate. Otherwise, they will fight vigorously to defend their land. If the contenders are evenly matched, the fight could go on for days and result in serious injury or death.[80]

A similar process occurs in social groups, whether it be among robins or other types of animals. The larger and stronger animals typically display aggression toward their subordinates for the purpose reinforcing their dominance. In this way, fighting is kept to a minimum because every animal knows its place in the group. Since the weakest animal is at the bottom of the ranking system, it will be dominated by every other animal. Instead of working together for the common good, survival of the fittest generally seems to rule the day.

A lowly shepherd who lives a solitary life among domesticated animals and various forms of wildlife may rightly ask, is man any better than the animal kingdom? Apparently not as much as he would like to think. Are not those medieval knights who jousted with lances on running horses comparable to big-horned sheep who run at full force against each other? Are not modern military jets similar to birds that fight to defend their territories from aggressors? Man's history is filled with accounts of war between families, tribes, ethnic groups, civil wars among citizens, and larger-scale wars among nations and countries. Short of bloodshed, tensions and animosities are not uncommon in the clamor for land, resources, or political domination.

But a shepherd also knows that many animals are known to display a desire to contribute toward the physical well-being of other biological creatures of the same or a different species. Herdsmen hold in high esteem large white guard dogs that instinctively live among their sheep and consider it their duty to protect them from predators, such as the Great Pyrenees that originated in France, the Akbash of Turkish origin, or the Komondor from Hungary. Dogs of various species protect humans and other animals, including the German shepherd, which is used by police and the military to provide a unique public service for which they are given much recognition.

Well-known news reports also indicate that dolphins are known to rescue humans from drowning or from sharks, keeping them safe from harm. New Zealanders once documented a pod of whales that ran aground during ebb-tide, and when the tide came back, a pod of dolphins herded the disoriented whales back out to sea, saving seventy-six out of eighty of them.[81]

Birds also have distinct predispositions to assist each other and to work for the common good of their community. Each year thousands of geese fly from Canada to the southern parts of the United States to escape Canada's bitter cold weather. In their migration, they gather in flocks forming a V-shaped flying pattern in order to provide an additional lift and a reduction of air resistance.[82] In this way they can fly further with the same amount of energy than if each goose flew alone. When the lead goose flying in the front of the formation gets tired of breaking the flow of the wind for the two lines of birds that follow, it will drop out of the lead, and another goose will take its place. As these flocks of birds travel across the sky, their distinct honking sound can be easily heard as they communicate with each other along their way. If one goose becomes ill or injured and drops out of the formation, two other geese will remain with the weakened goose to protect it from predators until it recovers or dies.

What, then, is a shepherd to determine when contrasting animals that display selfish dispositions from those who seem predisposed to protect others? Animals that are prone to prey on the weak may be said to confine their thinking to the lowest, or physical sphere, of intelligence: the survival of the fittest. Conversely, animals that demonstrate a desire to sacrifice their own safety or convenience for the protection of others may be considered to base their ambitions on a higher level of enlightenment.

This is not to say, however, that the moral capacities of animals are the same as those of human beings. Human beings are able to draw on the collective knowledge of humanity in a way that no animal can, sometimes referred to as collective cognition. But the basic idea is the same for both animals and humans: they can draw on their basic physical tendencies, or they can elevate themselves to a higher level or realm of existence.

Our Creator has endowed man with moral agency to use the natural resources as he sees fit, without any threat of force or coercion. To aid in his ambitions, He ordained that man should cultivate the earth and produce the various fruits, grains, and herbs for his use and benefit.[83] Grass, flowers, and trees were organized to grow freely. Land-roaming animals, fish in the waters, and birds in the air were all placed under man's dominion and control. Regardless of any genetic altering of plant and animal life over time, from the beginning these creations been designed to meet the essential needs of man but they also have been created in abundance to please the sight, the taste, and the smell of all who dwell here.

Given this remarkable gift, why does there exist widespread destitution and hunger? Why are there entire nations of poverty, misery, and distress? Why so much selfishness and hate, bloodshed and destruction? The person who knows and appreciates the laws by which this earth is governed will not find these questions difficult to answer. That person will understand that misuse of moral agency frustrates progress and confines its subjects to the lower, physical sphere of existence. Individuals, families, communities, and entire nations that adhere to this lower law that governs the physical sphere must of necessity recognize that their selfish acts will bring harsh consequences, for every seed brings forth fruit of its own kind.

The distinction between humans that prey on the weak as opposed to those that are prone to protect them is visible, not only individually but in family relations and even societies. The old proverb that "birds of a feather flock together" suggests that similar people tend to associate with each other. Those of similar tastes and ambitions congregate in groups. Those with sensual and carnal minds form gangs or similar groups designed to collectively carry out their sinister designs. Similarly, individuals with worthy ambitions congregate into charities, clubs, and religious organizations to collectively pursue wholesome and uplifting objectives. On the national level, self-centered political leaders seek to justify gross behavior on weaker members of society, such as the Nazi exploitations during the Holocaust, whereas other unselfish societies have sought to provide governmental relief to those in need.

Those who live amidst nature understand her law, which provides that every planted seed will eventually bring forth fruit of its own kind. Nature reminds us on a regular basis that dogs beget dogs, and cats beget cats. Their offspring remain within the boundaries that their Creator has ordained for them from the beginning. Trees do not reproduce into potatoes, and potato seeds will never produce ears of corn. The same law holds true among intangible things. Truth will embrace truth and mercy will seek after the merciful and lay claim on its own, whether it be as individuals, families, or entire nations. Likewise, injustice and corruption will breed fruit of its own kind. Nature's Creator governs and executes all things according to His just laws.

What, then, will become of those governmental institutions that plant within their legal framework seeds of justice and recognize basic God-given rights to life, liberty, and pursuit of happiness? Will such a system, if cultivated and maintained, spring forth a hundredfold into a social order that will provide continuing prosperity and happiness of its people, as is the lesson of seeds that are planted in nature's soil? And on the other hand, will the planting of undesirable seeds or failure to nurture good seeds produce misery and torment just as a garden that is not nourished and cultivated will produce an outcropping of undesirable weeds or barren soil?

Unlike the government of man, our Creator's system of governance in relation to this earth and the universe that surrounds it was designed to be an eternal, organized system of order and moral discipline, not a system of rebellion and corruption. Will our Creator's system prevail over those man-made systems of a lesser realm? As history unfolds, it remains the duty of all people to properly exercise moral agency, caring for the poor and the needy, attending to the needs of the sick and the afflicted, and dealing with others with integrity and restraint. When exercised properly, seeds will be planted that will ultimately produce those attributes that fulfill the measure of our creation and lead to never-ending lives of joy and happiness.

Endnotes:

66 Technically, to say that the Earth revolves around the sun is not exactly true. The earth, the sun, and all the planets within our solar system are orbiting around the center of mass of our solar system according to Ross Pomeroy, (Aug. 05, 2014) "Technically, Earth Does Not Orbit Around the Sun," RealClear Science." Retrieved from http://www.realclearscience.com/blog/2014/08/technically_the_earth_does_not_obit_the_sun.html.

67 Ibid.

68 Ibid., "Polar Star."

69 Genesis 3:17–19

70 This thought is set forth in Sill, Sterling W., *Our World of Wonders*, Bountiful, Utah: Horizon Publishers, 1986, 59.

71 Genesis 2:8

72 Genesis 2:19

73 Genesis 2:5–17

74 Genesis 3:9–19

75 See Kleinkopf, Westermann, Wille, and Kleinschmidt, "Specific Gravity of Russet Burbank Potatoes," *American Potato Journal*, Vol. 64, 1987.

76 Taylor, John, *Government of God,* S. W. Richards, London, England, 1852, 1.

77 Colossians 1:16–17

78 Psalm 8:3–6

79 While these observations are personal to the author, a general discussion of the behavior of Rambouillet rams can be found in reading Brown, Sheep Behavior Under Unherded Conditions on Mountain Summer Ranges, Utah Agricultural Experiment Station, Utah State University, July 3, 1970.

80 A general discussion pertaining to the behavior habits of robins is found in an undated article written by Russell Link, *Robins—Living with Wildlife,* Washington Department of Fish & Wildlife.

81 Such an experience was reported by Dolphins-World, *Dolphins Rescuing Humans,* Miami, Florida: Bio Expedition Publishing, January 28, 2014.

82 Library of Congress, "Why do geese fly in a V?," https://www.loc.gov/rr/scitech/misteries/geese.html.

83 Genesis 1:26–29

Lesson 15

A Sheepman's Last Words

The ranch kid home, his meal ahead,
      His youthful hands to butter bread
—A life's dream born, his blood pure red—
He licks his chops and goes to bed.

The herdsman home, his sheepdogs fed,
      He chucks his gloves and cracks his bread
—His life is worn, his blood beet red—
He soaks his corns and goes to bed.

The old boss home, his orders said,
      With calloused hands he breaks his bread
—His life forlorn, his blood dark red—
He cleans his teeth and goes to bed.

A frail sheep home but not quite dead,
      Her broken hoofs and teeth full spread
—Her life coat shorn, her blood still red—
Softly blows her nose and goes to bed.

Enough of earth, this life I've lead!
>No need to mourn as I gum my bread
—New life be born, no blood that's red—
I'll give up the ghost and go to bed.

My soul's back home, as the scripture said,
>With hopeful heart, my life's book read
—Our Lord adorn, for the blood He shed—
He heals my wounds, He prepares my bed.

The alternation of day and night demonstrates the order of life in which work and rest succeed one another in a beautiful display of harmony and regularity. The young ranch boy, eager and alert, begins his day full of vigor as he sets out to explore the world and cultivate his interests and talents. But at the end of the day, after the fierce heat of the sun has eased and softened into a restful glow, he is ready to settle back home, where he can find nourishment, leisure, and rest.

As the young boy matures, each morning he energetically leaves his home to do his assigned work, laboriously giving of himself with an honest day's effort and leaving no responsibility left unfulfilled. But then again, by the end of the day, as the sun falls, he feels that fatigue of body that summons him home for supper and a soft place to lay his head. The reward of his labor is the rest procured from a hard day's work, and the satisfaction of knowing that his rest has been rightfully earned.

With the passing of time, he finds that his entire life follows the same pattern that the span of a mere twenty-four hours has generated since childhood. Like the progressive rising of the sun, the enthusiasm of his youth, followed by the full strength of adulthood, is now at the height of his life. He leaves home each day with a sense of confidence that he can physically handle the work that lies ahead, and he returns with a strong appetite for food and rest as he contemplates what needs to be accomplished the next day.

But as the years progress, like the subtle falling of the sun, his vibrancy begins to wane, and he wearily comes home each evening with ever-increasing exhaustion, aches, and pains. But his mind remains sharp, and his increasing passion to come home is not merely for the ease and comfort that await him there but for the peace that serves as a warm homecoming following a hard and stressful day. Like the stillness that follows the tumult of a storm, his lifetime of achievements shine in the back of his mind like the stars that span the nightly heavens, some of which barely glimmer in the distant spaces of his mind.

Now an old man, he looks back on his life and realizes that his life has required both industry and obedience to achieve the satisfaction of a life well lived. He recalls that his Creator had emphasized the importance of work: "Cursed is the ground for thy sake."[84] He appreciates how work rewards leisure time, enhances self-esteem with a feeling of accomplishment, develops patience and faith in the pursuit of a desired outcome, and boosts one's ability to understand and appreciate others. Add in the ingredient of obedience, and the product is a strong and vibrant moral character, filled with satisfaction and the reward of accomplishment.

Looking back, the old man fully appreciates the importance of seeking more in his life than mere satisfaction of physical appetites and desires. He recognizes that his entry into the moral sphere of his mortal existence was a critical accomplishment along his pathway toward complete happiness, but as he sought to elevate himself even higher into the spiritual realm, he learned that this is where the full measure of his creation can be achieved. Looking back, he recognizes that although the pressures of the long hours of hard work and difficult tasks are now replaced with the aches and pains of old age, his life is void of unresolved regrets, and he is comforted with the assurance of a still, small voice that everything in his life is in order and that all is well.

It has been said that order is the first law of heaven. Better it might be said that obedience is the first law of heaven, for it was by obedience to the fixed laws of the universe that order was introduced in the heavens. The achievement of order requires work. Regardless, this first law is followed by a second, which is that everything in nature has a purpose.[85] Collectively, these two great laws sum up the existence of a successful and fulfilled life.

"But where do I stand in the eyes of my Creator?" the aged shepherd contemplates. "If the heavens and the earth were so marvelously created by that first great law of heaven, which is obedience, is it not likewise true that my life is placed in proper order through obedience to those immutable laws of nature? And if I was created in obedience to those fixed laws of the universe, should I not also exercise my agency by striving to be obedient to those natural laws my Creator has commanded me to obey, thereby enabling me to progress from the physical realm of carnal instincts to the moral sphere where the honorable men of the earth reside? And can I not then continue to progress as I continue to refine my moral conduct through my spiritual senses?"

The shepherd further contemplates the second law of heaven and asks, "What is my purpose on earth? By hearkening to the words of my Creator and exercising faith in Him, might I not only be redeemed of physical death and decay like every other seed brings forth fruit of its own kind but also redeemed of spiritual death by becoming His seed through my obedience, that I might be born again into His kingdom as opposed to some less-desirable location? Or if I fail to be obedient, is it not likewise true that I might find my life out of order and fall short of the purpose for which I was placed on this earth? Will I fail in the ultimate purpose for which I was created?"

He then concludes, "It all comes down to my obedience in obeying the laws and commands of my Creator. Everything I have done in my life that was worth pursuing, not fully knowing beforehand the eventual outcome, has required me to exercise patience and faith." He is then again reminded, "With everything in nature so well planned and organized, it must have required faith and obedience to bring order to all created things, and so too will I exercise my faith by repenting of my shortcomings and completing the term of my mortal existence in strict obedience to God's law. Regardless of the mistakes of my past, I may ultimately be entitled to rest from my labors and find peace and comfort in going home to the house of God, my Creator."

The aged shepherd has no fear of death as he contemplates his future. The lessons he has learned from the environment into which he was born have given him a sure conviction that his Creator is a professional in conducting the affairs of His business, and he feels the love and assurance from his Creator that everything in his life has been perfectly planned and organized through obedience to the laws that govern the universe, of which he is a part.

The shepherd concludes his life with words of gratitude for his Creator. Who is this great Creator? The Lord Jesus Christ is that supreme being who was called upon by His Father to come to this earth and inhabit a mortal body of flesh and bone, who died an ignominious death at the hands of men who would kill their own God, but who then had the capacity to rise from the dead and bring all mortality with Him.

Salvation is centered in the Lord Jesus Christ. His atoning sacrifice is the single-most-important event that has occurred in the history of all created things. The great plan of salvation was created by our heavenly Father, that same being who created us and to whom we owe our existence. And it was our heavenly Father's Son, Jesus Christ, born of a mortal mother named Mary, who accepted the call to redeem us from our mortal, corruptible state. It is to Jesus Christ to whom we directly express our gratitude for immortality and eternal life.

Meanwhile, from the day of our birth until our dying breath that small voice beckons us on:

> *"Only be thou strong . . . and of good courage;*
> *be not afraid, neither be thou dismayed: for*
> *. . . thy God is with thee whithersoever thou*
> *goest."[86]*

Endnotes:

84 Genesis 3:17

85 Talmadge, James E., *First Book of Nature*, Salt Lake City, Utah: The Contributor Company, 1888, 265.

86 Joshua 1:7–9

Printed in the United States
By Bookmasters